Biblical
Road to
BLESSING

Biblical
Road to
BLESSING

BENNY HINN

THOMAS NELSON PUBLISHERS
Nashville • Atlanta • London • Vancouver

Dedication

Dedicated to the love of my life,
my lovely "help meet"
SUZANNE,
who is both God's greatest blessing to me,
and my partner together
on the Biblical Road to Blessing.

Acknowledgments

I am again grateful to Rick Nash and Sheryl Palmquist for their editorial assistance in developing this manuscript. Also, Roy Harthern worked to summarize material on this topic.

Contents

I Expect a Miracle Today!

For with God, nothing is impossible!
It's not possible to be impossible.
And with God, every promise shall come true,
For we know surely all things He can do.

There's healing in the name of Jesus,
Healing in the touch of Jesus.
One touch of His hand will lift you,
Body, mind and soul.

Believe Him, for His power can free you.
Praise Him, for His mercies toward you.
Thank Him, for His love: He longs to make you
fully whole.

Just one touch of the Master's hand,
Just one word—He has full command.
Have faith in what He wants to do is all He asks
of you.

Believe Him, for His power can free you.
Praise Him, for His mercies toward you.

Thank Him, for His love: He longs to make you
fully whole.

I expect a miracle today!
Nothing is impossible for those who believe and say:
I believe God's Word is still the same.
I expect a miracle today.[1]

The words of this wonderful song so express the expectation I feel in my heart and the reality the blessed Holy Spirit lets me experience every day—I *expect* a miracle today! And the reason is simple: God's Word *is* still the same! God hasn't changed, and He hasn't stopped working. In fact, through the work of the Holy Spirit, we have the opportunity to see greater works than ever before. It is just as the Scripture declares, "Most assuredly, I say to you, he who believes in Me, the works that I do he will do also; and greater *works* than these he will do, because I go to My Father." (John 14:12)

My friend, there has never been a greater time to be alive than right now! The same things recorded in the book of Acts are taking place before our very eyes because the same Holy Spirit is at work today as was manifest in the book of Acts. Glorious things happened in the days of Paul the apostle and the disciples who walked with the Master. Many times I have heard men and women of the church reflect fondly upon the times gone by, wishing they could have been a part of them. But I believe we are standing at the threshold of the greatest days in the history of the church. And we are about to step into such an outpouring of supernatural power that, if given the opportunity, Paul would say, "I wish I could be a part of what's happening in the nineties in your cities and churches!"

The Holy Spirit's Work

The early church of the book of Acts experienced abundant life in its fullness. And just as in the book of Acts, three things are about to happen when the Holy Spirit begins to work in all of His wonderful power.

1. People Will Be Saved (Acts 2)

When the Holy Spirit fell at Pentecost, Peter was transformed into a fearless preacher of truth. Preaching to the assembled crowd on that day with a boldness birthed of the Spirit, Peter was uncompromising in his message:

> "Therefore let all the house of Israel know assuredly that God has made this Jesus, whom you crucified, both Lord and Christ." Now when they heard this, they were cut to the heart, and said to Peter and the rest of the apostles, "Men and brethren, what shall we do?" Then Peter said to them, "Repent, and let every one of you be baptized in the name of Jesus Christ for the remission of sins; and you shall receive the gift of the Holy Spirit." "For the promise is to you and to your children, and to all who are afar off, as many as the Lord our God will call." . . . Then those who gladly received his word were baptized; and that day about three thousand souls were added to them. (Acts 2:36–39, 41)

Today people are responding to the message of the gospel in record numbers. They are experiencing forgiveness and a fresh start through a personal relationship with the Lord Jesus Christ, and God is calling people of faith to bold, ambitious exploits for Him more than ever before. Recently, while in Puerto Rico, Dr. Billy Graham preached to nearly a *billion* people at one time through satellite. We are seeing evangelism on a worldwide scale. The Lord is speaking to men of God such as Dr. Bill Bright and Pat Robertson to reach *millions* of souls before the year 2000. An incredible move of evangelism has begun.

In many of our own international crusades, the Holy Spirit is drawing more than 500,000 people for a single service. In Japan, where just .05 percent of the population is Christian, we are seeing more people gather for Christian meetings there than ever before in the history of that country. With the collapse of communism, the Holy Spirit has poured into the formerly Marxist countries like a rushing, mighty wind.

Recently it has been my privilege to pray with a number of world leaders—some of whom were previously well-known for their resistance to the gospel. As I reflect on this, I can't help but be overwhelmed with gratitude to God that He let me live to witness the day when leaders who were once closed to the gospel are now receptive to the Lord's claims by the power of the Holy Spirit.

Please don't misunderstand. I don't share these things to brag about our ministry. I mention them merely to put an exclamation point on this irrefutable fact: there is an amazing move of the Holy Spirit for evangelism taking place today. It is crossing all boundaries and is reaching from the "guttermost to the uttermost!"

2. People Will Be Healed (Acts 3)

When the Holy Spirit is truly at work, evangelism and healing will always be found, each pointing to and setting the stage for the other. In Acts 2, three thousand people came to the Savior in a single day. Just think of it! The effect on Jerusalem was electric. All eyes were on the leaders of the mighty movement:

> Now Peter and John went up together to the temple at the hour of prayer, the ninth hour. And a certain man lame from his mother's womb was carried, whom they laid daily at the gate of the temple which is called Beau-

tiful, to ask alms from those who entered the temple; who, seeing Peter and John about to go into the temple, asked for alms. And fixing his eyes on him, with John, Peter said, "Look at us." So he gave them his attention, expecting to receive something from them. Then Peter said, "Silver and gold I do not have, but what I do have I give you: In the name of Jesus Christ of Nazareth, rise up and walk." And he took him by the right hand and lifted him up, and immediately his feet and ankle bones received strength. So he, leaping up, stood and walked and entered the temple with them—walking, leaping, and praising God. And all the people saw him walking and praising God. Then they knew that it was he who sat begging alms at the Beautiful Gate of the temple; and they were filled with wonder and amazement at what had happened to him. (Acts 3:1–10)

So healing followed evangelism. But notice very carefully: Peter used the healing that captured the public's attention to preach the gospel to them:

Now as the lame man who was healed held on to Peter and John, all the people ran together to them in the porch which is called Solomon's, greatly amazed. So when Peter saw it, he responded to the people: "Men of Israel, why do you marvel at this? Or why look so intently at us, as though by our own power or godliness we had made this man walk? The God of Abraham, Isaac, and Jacob, the God of our fathers, glorified His Servant Jesus, whom you delivered up and denied in the presence of Pilate, when he was determined to let Him go. But you denied the Holy One and the Just, and asked for a murderer to be granted to you, and killed the Prince of life, whom God raised from the dead, of which we are witnesses. And His name, through faith in His name, has made this man strong, whom you see and know. Yes, the faith which comes through Him has given him this perfect soundness in the presence of you all. Yet now, brethren, I know that you did it in ignorance, as did also your rulers. But those things which God foretold by the mouth of all His prophets, that the Christ would suffer, He has thus fulfilled. Repent therefore and be converted, that your sins may be blotted out, so that times of refreshing may come from the presence of the Lord, and that He may send Jesus Christ, who was preached to you before, whom heaven must receive until the times of restoration of all things, which God has spoken by the mouth of all His holy prophets since the world began." (Acts 3:11–21)

Yes, healing and evangelism always go together, working hand in hand—and today we are seeing more evidence of the Master's healing touch than ever before. Yes, God's Word is *still* the same. Scripture records that God healed all the people when they came out of Egypt, for Psalm 105:37 declares:

He also brought them out with silver and gold,
And there was none feeble among His tribes.

The blessed Master often healed all who were around Him, for Luke noted in Acts 10:38: "God anointed Jesus of Nazareth with the Holy Spirit and with power, who went about doing good and healing all who were oppressed by the devil, for God was with Him."

Miracles of this magnitude are not only still possible, but *they are happening today*. Kathryn Kuhlman prophesied that the day would come when we would see everyone healed in a service or services. And this prophecy will come to pass because it's God's Word. God is not a respecter of persons; if He healed all once, He can do it again. It is the promise of His Holy Word.

This incredible move of healing will come. Isaiah wrote most plainly of that quickly coming day, predicting:

> Then the eyes of the blind shall be opened,
> And the ears of the deaf shall be unstopped.
> Then the lame shall leap like a deer,
> And the tongue of the dumb sing.
> For waters shall burst forth in the wilderness,
> And streams in the desert. . . .
> No lion shall be there,
> Nor shall any ravenous beast go up on it;
> It shall not be found there.
> But the redeemed shall walk there,
> And the ransomed of the LORD shall return,
> And come to Zion with singing,
> With everlasting joy on their heads.
> They shall obtain joy and gladness,
> And sorrow and sighing shall flee away.
> (Isa. 35: 5–6, 9–10)

People Will Experience "No Lack" (Acts 4)

First there was salvation (Acts 2), then there was healing (Acts 3), and then there was a most wonderful blessing of the Father that Acts 4 refers to as "no lack." As the gospel continued to be preached with resolute authority, the three thousand who surrendered to Jesus the Messiah quickly grew to more than eight thousand (Acts 4:4), and later multitudes were saved as the Scripture clearly states. The power of the proclamation of the gospel was again accompanied by a mighty manifestation of miracle-working power after they had prayed, saying:

> "Now, Lord, look on their threats, and grant to Your servants that with all boldness they may speak Your word, by stretching out Your hand to heal, and that signs and wonders may be done through the name of Your holy

Servant Jesus." And when they had prayed, the place
where they were assembled together was shaken; and
they were all filled with the Holy Spirit, and they spoke
the word of God with boldness." (Acts 4:29–31)

How exciting it must have been to live in those days—
almost as exciting as it is to be living in these days! But pay
careful attention here. Immediately following this is an extremely significant insight, one that is often overlooked or
misunderstood, for the Word of God declares:

Now the multitude of those who believed were of one
heart and one soul; neither did anyone say that any of
the things he possessed was his own, but they had all
things in common. And with great power the apostles
gave witness to the resurrection of the Lord Jesus. And
great grace was upon them all. *Nor was there anyone
among them who lacked*; for all who were possessors of
lands or houses sold them, and brought the proceeds of
the things that were sold, and laid them at the apostles'
feet; and they distributed to each as anyone had need.
(Acts 4:32–35, emphasis added)

In the midst of the mighty manifestation of the saving
and healing power of the Lord Jesus, our heavenly Father
provided for those saints such that they *never lacked*. As they
surrendered to the God who had saved them and healed
them, that same God *prospered* them and they experienced
no lack. And God's Word is the same today. The same God
who wants to *save* you wants to *heal* you. And the same God
who wants to *heal* you wants to *bless* you.

For more than twenty years, our wonderful Lord Jesus
has given me the privilege of taking His saving and healing
message literally around the world through crusades, on
television, in the pulpit of a local church, through the In-
ternet, and through books. What joy I have known as I have

taught about the person and work of the Holy Spirit, His anointing, and the blood of our dear Savior!

But just as the Father has deposited within me a passion to preach the good news to the lost and to pray that the sick might be healed, so now at this crucial hour He has placed within me an urgency to share with the body of Christ how each and every one of us can experience no lack, that is, *true biblical prosperity*.

Biblical Blessing: The Need of the People

Let me explain why I sense that this is *the* critical hour to teach on the biblical road to blessing. The first reason is my concern that so many brothers and sisters in the Lord are missing out on the life of blessing that our loving heavenly Father longs to bestow on all of His children.

In our ministry we are resolutely committed to prayer, and each week fully two-thirds of the calls and letters we receive request prayer for financial breakthrough. Think of it—thousands upon thousands of people each and every week request prayer for financial needs alone. And this number is representative of thousands more who have the same needs but who don't contact us.

Not that this should come as any surprise, I suppose. A poll in *U.S. News & World Report* focused on the relative happiness of Americans with various aspects of their lives. On a scale of 1 through 10, with 1 being lowest and 10 being highest, Americans gave their happiness with their financial situation a score of 5.98. Any score lower than 7 was deemed to denote "relative unhappiness."[2]

As I write this book in mid-1996, it seems that every day I hear reports on radio and television and read them in the newspapers about how Americans are more extended on credit than ever before—almost certainly overextended, and barely able to make even the minimum payments. They are experiencing what the Bible states emphatically about debt:

> The rich rules over the poor,
> And the borrower is servant to the lender.
> (Prov. 22:7)

Furthermore, so much of the increasing stress in our culture goes right back to financial issues. We try to support a style of living apart from surrender to God only to find that we're ground up trying to make it work. A story in *Marriage Partnership* magazine encapsulated the problem this way:

> When researchers ask married couples what they argue about, money always ranks near the top of the list. If you're like most couples, money problems disrupt your marriage as much as disagreements over [anything else]. It's not uncommon for spouses to feel that financial pressures are pushing them beyond their limit.[3]

But underneath these issues may be an even larger problem, one to which the prophet Haggai admonished us to pay close attention:

> Now this is what the LORD Almighty says: "Give careful thought to your ways. You have planted much, but have harvested little. You eat, but never have enough. You drink, but never have your fill. You put on clothes, but are not warm. You earn wages, only to put them in a purse with holes in it." This is what the LORD Almighty says: "Give careful thought to your ways. Go up into the mountains and bring down timber and build the house [i.e., the temple of the LORD], so that I may take pleasure in it and be honored," says the LORD. "You expected much, but see, it turned out to be little. What

you brought home, I blew away. Why?'' declares the LORD Almighty. "Because of my house, which remains a ruin, while each of you is busy with his own house. Therefore, because of you the heavens have withheld their dew and the earth its crops. I called for a drought on the fields and the mountains, on the grain, the new wine, the oil and whatever the ground produces, on men and cattle, and on the labor of your hands." Then Zerubbabel son of Shealtiel, Joshua son of Jehozadak, the high priest, and the whole remnant of the people obeyed the voice of the LORD their God and the message of the prophet Haggai, because the LORD their God had sent him. And the people feared the LORD. (1:5–12 NIV)

Haggai's words stand in sharp contrast to the promises noted in Malachi 3:

"Bring all the tithes into the storehouse,
That there may be food in My house,
And try Me now in this,"
Says the LORD of hosts,
"If I will not open for you the windows of heaven
And pour out for you such blessing
That there will not be room enough to receive it.
And I will rebuke the devourer for your sakes,
So that he will not destroy the fruit of your ground,
Nor shall the vine fail to bear fruit for you in the
    field,"
Says the LORD of hosts;
"And all nations will call you blessed,
For you will be a delightful land,"
Says the LORD of hosts. (vv. 10–12)

My dear friend, I know that like my desire the earnest desire of your heart is to have the experience described by Malachi, not the futility described by Haggai, and this is why

I have been led of God to write this book, *The Biblical Road to Blessing*. You can experience freedom from financial bondage, and I want to show you how.

Biblical Blessing: The Need of the Church

We are witnessing the greatest move of evangelism in the history of humankind, the most spectacular works of healing. The blessed Holy Spirit is working as never before. We have more open doors, more opportunities, more ways to spread the Word, and more people willing to commit their lives to spreading the gospel than ever before. The chance to impact the entire world for the Master is greater than it has ever been.

Yet an obstacle remains—an obstacle that is more formidable than government persecution, more fundamental than satanic opposition. It is the lack of surrender in the area of giving in the lives of some of God's people. The Master calls for each of His children to give back at least 10 percent of income for the work of the gospel. Yet statistics reveal that far, far too many of God's people are missing the biblical blessing that comes from giving.

- One Southern Baptist official reports, "I have found that in a majority of churches, more like 12 percent give 80 percent of the money, and 50 percent of the members give nothing."[4]
- A study by the Independent Sector on giving and volunteering in the United States reported that overall contributions to charitable causes declined 10 percent (in constant 1993 dollars) between 1987 and 1993.[5]
- Households with incomes below $10,000 give away an average of 2.8 percent of their income, while households with income between $50,000 and $100,000 give away only 1.5 percent. Nearly half of the total contributions to charity in the U.S. comes

from households with incomes below $30,000, a study found.[6]

Think of it—we are living in the greatest potential time of harvest in the history of the world, and 50 percent or more of God's people are giving nothing at all! We are living in a time of unparalleled spiritual openness and unprincipled satanic deception, yet God's people are not giving even 3 percent of their income to carry the light. If anything, O. S. Hawkins is understating the case when he says:

> The principal hindrance to the advancement of the Kingdom of God is greed. It is the chief obstacle to heaven-sent revival. It seems that when the back of greed is broken, the human spirit soars into regions of unselfishness. I believe it is safe to say there can be no continuous revival without "hilarious" giving. And I fear no contradiction: wherever there is "hilarious" giving there will soon be revival![7]

I believe that the vast majority of God's people want to tithe. They know that it's right. They don't need to be convinced of its truth so much as they need to be encouraged that they can actually do it: that 90 percent with God's blessing will go much farther than 100 percent without it.

But too many people are buried by debt, overwhelmed by responsibilities, gripped by fears. As a result, they sincerely don't know how to break the cycle and experience the blessing that comes from biblical giving. Can I let you in on a secret? As a young Christian, neither did I. Like so many, I was overloaded with debt and harried by fear; I simply didn't know what the Word of God said about how to start on the way of blessing He intends for each believer. In this book, I'm going to share the same transforming principles God revealed to me. And I'm confident that as a result, there will be more resources to take the saving and healing message of the Savior around the world.

Biblical Blessing: Much More Than You May Think

God's blessing is about so much more than material riches. People who focus on material riches to the exclusion of the rest of God's blessings limit God and fail to notice the veritable myriad of ways that He blesses us moment by moment. Now having said that, I have to agree with something I heard Zig Ziglar say once to a group of people: "I've been poor, and I've been rich. And let me tell you, it's better to be rich!"

After the audience stopped laughing, he went on to make a crucial point:

> Money will buy a bed but not sleep;
> books but not brains;
> food but not appetite;
> finery but not beauty;
> a house but not a home;
> medicine but not health;
> luxuries but not culture;
> amusements but not happiness;
> religion but not salvation.

Riches are beside the point, for the Scriptures affirm that "godliness with contentment is great gain." (1 Tim. 6:6) Without *contentment*, you will never have enough. With contentment, you can experience joy in the most desolate areas on earth. Riches will not bring happiness. Obedience brings happiness, for Solomon himself plainly declares:

> A man can do nothing better than to eat and drink and find satisfaction in his work. *This too, I see, is from the hand of God, for without him, who can eat or find enjoyment?* To the man who pleases him, God gives wisdom, knowledge and happiness, but to the sinner he gives the task of gathering and storing up wealth to hand it over to

the one who pleases God. This too is meaningless, a chasing after the wind. (Eccl. 2:24–26 NIV)

Yet having said this, I must point out that it is also a mistake to presume that God doesn't care about our financial well-being or that His promises of blessing include the spiritual but not the financial. R. T. Kendall has a penetrating insight here:

> These promises [of Mal. 3:10–11] point to a *material* return as one kind of blessing from the Lord. Obviously some will prosper more than others, owing to gifts, place of responsibility, or opportunity. But *at the bottom* of it all is a promise for *all* believers that they will be honored even at a material level in such a way that, whether it be more or less than others, it is more than it would have been had they not been faithful in Christian stewardship. There are countless testimonies that could be brought forward that tell of financial hardships, debt and distress, until tithing was begun. Not that such people became millionaires or drove Rolls-Royces, but they lived without the terror of constant financial adversity.[8]

When we experience the wonderful blessing described in the Scripture as "no lack," each day is an adventure as we find our loving heavenly Father meeting our needs and so much more in ways that we would never have anticipated. But not only do we experience the adventure of having our own needs met, we get to experience the blessing of responding to the leading of the Holy Spirit to meet the needs of others. In this way we experience the truth so magnificently summarized by Matthew Henry: "The riches we impart are the only wealth we shall always retain."[9]

The Biblical Road to Blessing: Much Different from What You May Think

I am writing this book because of the human need that I see all around me and the opportunity that exists to take the gospel to the world—but I am also writing because there is so much *mis*understanding about the blessings of God. *The Bible does not teach the sort of theology that is often called "name it and claim it."* Actually, I prefer to call it "blab it and grab it"! I want to state this very plainly so that there is no misunderstanding: if you are reading this book to learn how to get rich, you are not only starting in the wrong place, *you are reading the wrong book!*

You see, the biblical road to blessing is not an infomercial. There is no 800 number to call, and our sovereign God isn't Aladdin. The Bible is not a witches' spell book full of formulas that allow us to manipulate God to do what we want. The Bible is not a catalog that we use to pick out what we want and then await delivery.

No, first and foremost the word of God is a *love story*. It tells of the amazing, steadfast, loyal love of our heavenly Father. And in the Bible, we learn how we can live daily in a love relationship with Him. We learn how to experience Him for what He is—our Father—and how we can live as obedient, happy children.

So you see, the biblical road to blessing isn't about formulas or even heavy doctrine. No, it's about how to fall in love with God the Father. It's about how to let the Father meet your every need—including financial. It's about a life more fulfilling and satisfying than you ever thought possible. It's the biblical road to blessing, and I invite you to join me.

CHAPTER 9

The Loving, Giving Father

The pale golden glow from the lamp gently warmed the room with its light. Seated in a comfortable chair with my son, Joshua, on my lap, I relaxed for a few moments, musing over the activities of the day. Down the hallway I could hear the familiar sounds of Jessica and Natasha getting ready for bed. Eleasha, our youngest daughter, was already asleep.

As the house grew quiet, Joshua snuggled closer to me. It was getting late, and even a boy with my son's considerable energy gets tired. The activities in the other part of the house faded into the distance as I continued to rehearse in my mind the events of the day.

When I finally concluded my reflecting, I glanced down at Joshua and noticed that he was fast asleep in my arms. He looked so peaceful lying there—almost angelic. As I sat there in the still of the night watching him sleep, he moved his head slightly, attempting to get more comfortable. When he changed his position, his chestnut brown hair shimmered in the subtle light. I stroked Joshua's hair gently as he slept. *How I cherish times like this with my children*, I thought as I lovingly touched his hair. *What a wonderful gift from the Lord!*

I don't know how long I sat there savoring the moment, but my heart was bubbling over with love for Josh and his

sisters, who by now were sound asleep down the hall. I
looked down at Josh's face and beheld such innocence and
total trust as he lay asleep in Daddy's arms. And the love
that I felt for him at that moment was beyond description.

My son, my Joshua, I thought as I brushed his cascading
hair back from his face. *My only boy . . . how I love him.
There's* nothing *in the world that I wouldn't give this boy . . .*
nothing *I wouldn't do for him or any of my children . . .* nothing *he could ever do to make me stop loving him or make me feel
differently toward him. Even when I must discipline him, my love*
never *changes.* I felt an overwhelming outpouring of unquenchable love for my son.

While I continued to stroke his head gently, basking in
the beauty of the priceless moment, the Lord whispered,
"What are your feelings toward your son right now?"

Although I recognized His still, small voice, I was startled by the question. Again the gentle voice of the Master
said softly, "Can you describe what you are feeling right
now?"

I struggled to find the right words and finally replied,
"No, Master, I can't begin to put it into words. The depth
and dimension of my love for my son are beyond description."

"Benny," the Lord said, "what you're feeling can't even
be compared to the love I have for you. It's only a tiny drop
in the ocean by comparison. It's a weak and worldly example of what I feel toward you. My love for you is so full of
kindness—My kindness so full of love. My love is steadfast,
unselfish, unchangeable, and endless. My love for you
never, ever fails."

In that tender moment, as I held my sleeping child in
my arms, the love that I felt as a father was so rich. But as
the Lord spoke to my heart, comparing the love I felt
toward Joshua with the greatness of His tender love for me,
I understood how weak and frail my love for my son was

when compared to God the Father's infinite love for us His children.

As a father, there is nothing that I would not do for my Jessica, Natasha, Joshua, or Eleasha. Nothing could make me stop loving them or forsake my commitment to them as their father. But my love for them, along with my ability and willingness to lovingly provide and care for my children, cannot begin to compare with the wonderful, loyal love that our heavenly Father has for you and me—a love that has never been more in evidence than it was on Calvary.

The Ultimate Gift of Love

The very nature and character of God are revealed through His ultimate act of giving when He offered His Son, Jesus Christ, as the supreme sacrifice for humankind. As a father, I cannot even begin to fathom the pain that our wonderful heavenly Father endured by allowing His Son to die the terrible death of Calvary.

I do everything in my power to prevent anything bad from happening to my children. I'm concerned when they have a bad day at school or when they scrape a knee while playing. Oh, how the Father's heart must have ached as He watched His precious, perfect Son rejected by the people He came to save, spat upon, scourged, sliced with a crown of thorns, and crucified among criminals and curs!

Oh, my friend, never doubt for even one moment the precious love of our wonderful heavenly Father for you and me. Truly, there is no other single greater thing that the Father could do to demonstrate His love for us than send His Son to die in our place and for our sins. As much as He grieved at the suffering inflicted upon Jesus, the thought of men and women spending eternity in hell grieved Him even more. No greater gift has ever been given, nor has such love been equaled in all of history.

Yet if the Father sacrificed so much to make a way for us to partake of eternal life with Him, does it make sense that a

God of such love would stop there in wanting to bless His children? The apostle Paul's clarion answer is as compelling today as it was in the first century:

> If God is for us, *who* can be against us? He who did not spare His own Son, but delivered Him up for us all, how shall He not with Him also freely give us all things? Who shall bring a charge against *God's* elect? It is God who justifies. Who is he who condemns? It is Christ who died, and furthermore is also risen, who is even at the right hand of God, who also makes intercession for us. Who shall separate us from the love of Christ? Shall tribulation, or distress, or persecution, or famine, or nakedness, or peril, or sword? As it is written:
> "For Your sake we are killed all day long;
> We are accounted as sheep for the slaughter."
> Yet in all these things we are more than conquerors through Him who loved us. For I am *persuaded* that neither death nor life, nor angels nor principalities nor powers, nor things present nor things to come, nor height nor depth, nor any other created thing, shall be able to separate us from the love of God which is in Christ Jesus our Lord. (Rom. 8:31b–39, emphasis added)

I have heard Dr. Oral Roberts often say, "God is a good God!" What could be more true? For I know that like me, you have experienced God's goodness in many ways and at many times. In fact, every good thing in our lives is a direct gift from our loving heavenly Father, as James 1:17 boldly states, "*Every* good gift and *every* perfect gift is from above, and comes down from the Father of lights, with whom there is *no variation or shadow of turning*" (emphasis added).

My dear friend, I desire so earnestly for you to begin to understand the love of our heavenly Father, to be *persuaded* by Him as the apostle Paul was. More than caring for you, our Father wants to bless you in every area of your life. The Word of God has much to say about His desire to bless you. And although salvation and eternal life represent the greatest blessings He could ever give, He is also concerned about every other area of your life.

Blessings from the Father

David proclaimed:

> Blessed be the Lord,
> *Who daily loads us with benefits,*
> The God of our salvation! (Ps. 68:19, emphasis added)

God wants to bless His children. As a father, I love to give gifts to my children and provide for them. And nothing brings me greater joy than to see the twinkle in their eyes as they unwrap a gift or to hear them giggle with delight as I give them something they have desired.

If a mere human being like me can find such joy through giving gifts to my children, just imagine how much joy our heavenly Father receives when He bestows good gifts upon us. Truly, our loving heavenly Father longs to bless His children—if for no other reason than for the pure joy of knowing the pleasure *we* receive when He provides for us.

How easy it can be to miss this very simple principle: God loves you and wants the very best for you. *He really does.* The Lord Jesus drives home this point so forcefully as to remove any doubt whatsoever about the Father's love toward us:

> "Ask, and it will be given to you; seek and you will find; knock, and it will be opened to you. For everyone who asks receives, and he who seeks finds, and to him who knocks it will be opened. Or what man is there among you who, if his son asks for bread, will give him a stone? Or if he asks for a fish, will he give him a serpent? If you

then, being evil, know how to give good gifts to your children, how much more will your Father who is in heaven give good things to those who ask Him! (Matt. 7:7–11)

In this wonderful passage the Savior declares that our heavenly Father *always* gives His children *good* gifts. And I'm so grateful because often without realizing it, we can ask for gifts that seem to be good but, in fact, are anything but.

Ice Cream, Please!

"I want ice cream, Daddy!"

"Eat your supper first, Joshua, and then you can have some ice cream." It was the beginning of a conversation with my son, Joshua, one evening as he and I enjoyed a meal together.

"I want ice cream, Daddy!"

"Eat your supper first, Joshua," I repeated, "and then you can have some ice cream. You can't have the ice cream until you eat your supper."

Joshua sat there, looking first at his dinner plate and then back at me. After some time, and a battle of the wills, he picked up his fork and began to eat the food before him. As he chewed his food slowly, he glanced at me from time to time, seemingly trying to determine how serious I was about his eating his dinner.

He was rather quiet as he ate his food, not his normal talkative self. He ate his food unenthusiastically, tiny bite by tiny bite. To encourage him, I reminded him about the delicious ice cream waiting for him in the freezer.

When he finally finished, he triumphantly showed me his empty plate and, with dazzling eyes and a smile that stretched across his entire face, said, "Ice cream, Daddy! I want ice cream!"

It gave me so much joy to hand him a generous bowlful of the ice cream I had promised. I was thrilled that he had obeyed me, and now I could bless him with dessert.

Several days later as I reflected on it, I realized that my evening experience with Joshua and the ice cream held rich insights regarding our relationship with our heavenly Father and His willingness to bless His children. Isn't it amazing how God designed the relationship between parents and children to give us an idea of His love and care for us? From the first moment Joshua looked at me with his beautiful dark eyes and asked for the ice cream, I absolutely wanted to give it to him because I knew how much he wanted it. However, as his father, I had a responsibility for his well-being. I knew how important it was for him to have the proper nourishment of a balanced meal, for while the main course is rarely as enticing as the dessert, it is almost always more beneficial.

But when Joshua finally ate that last morsel, held up his empty plate, and said, "Ice cream, Daddy! I want ice cream!" I was delighted to fulfill my promise and give him a big bowl of his favorite treat.

That's how our Father in heaven operates. He will satisfy our desires when we obey Him. My son had a desire for ice cream, but I knew that he really needed a balanced meal. I wanted to give Joshua his desired dessert, but he needed to obey me first concerning his need. After Joshua obeyed, I was delighted to give him plenty of ice cream.

This is just how our loving heavenly Father relates to us. We read in Scripture:

Delight yourself also in the LORD,
And He shall give you the desires of your heart.
(Ps. 37:4)

When we delight in Him, He gives us the desires that are submitted to His lordship. And since our heavenly Father rules over all without limitation, He delights to send wonderful blessings to His children when we obey Him.

A Father's Love

As a father, I love my children with every atom of my being. Each one is special, and I know that God has made them unique individuals.

My Jessica is so dear to me. I'm so proud of her, and she has grown to be such a lovely young lady. Sometimes I tease her about looking just like me. She always says to me with a twinkle in her beautiful, dark eyes, "Remember, I'm English, too, like Mom!"

And Natasha—well, she is something else. She is so alive and always tells me exactly what she thinks. If she has an opinion on something, she doesn't hesitate to let me know about it. She prefers to avoid attention publicly, saying as little as possible, but privately, she doesn't hold much back.

Now when it comes to Joshua, I'm never quite sure what to expect. He is always ready to accept a microphone and say hello or sing a song. I wonder where he gets that from? And I must say that the hello is much more predictable than the song. During one December crusade, he decided that he wanted to sing a song. He came to the platform and said his hellos to the people. When I asked him what he wanted to sing, he said, "Dashing Through the Snow." I wasn't successful at changing his mind to something spiritual such as "Silent Night," so instead he sang "Dashing Through the Snow."

Eleasha is our youngest daughter, and what a sweetheart she is! She is such a peaceful child and such a joy. My wife, Suzanne, and I can hardly remember a time when she has cried for any reason. No matter what is happening, she is basically happy about it. When it's time for bed, she just lies down, closes her eyes, and goes to sleep. No protest, no tears, just "night, night." And how she loves her brother! They are inseparable.

As you can tell, I could go on and on, filling page after page with stories about the special things that endear each of my children to my heart because I love them so. But I realize that as their father no matter how much I love each of them, my love for them is nothing in comparison to the love that God the Father has for you and me.

For example, what father do you know who would count every hair on his child's head? That night as Joshua lay sleeping in my lap, I certainly didn't attempt to count his every strand of hair. Yet our heavenly Father's love toward us is so consuming, so complete, that Scripture reveals that "the very hairs of [our heads] are all numbered." (Matt. 10:30)

I once heard Kathryn Kuhlman tell a story about going to her father, asking for things that she deeply desired. Although he didn't have the necessary funds to provide what she desired at the moment, her father loved her so much, he was determined to get them for her. He eventually borrowed the money to get the items she wanted. He was willing to do whatever was necessary just to bring joy to her.

If a natural father will go to such lengths and is so motivated for his child, just think of how much more God the Father is concerned for His children, for He loves us deeply!

Promised Blessings Throughout Scripture, we find many references to God's willingness and earnest desire to bless His children. There are so many verses regarding God's blessings to you and me that if I included all of them here, this book would become an encyclopedia. But I do want to share a few Scriptures to help you understand just how much God wants to bless His children in every area of life: both in the natural realm and in the spiritual realm. And because you are a believer, many of these blessings are promised to you and your children:

For I will pour water on him who is thirsty,
And floods on the dry ground;

I will pour My Spirit on your descendants,
And My blessing on your offspring. (Isa. 44:3)

It is like the dew of Hermon,
Descending upon the mountains of Zion;
For there the LORD commanded the blessing—
Life forevermore. (Ps. 133:3)

The nation of Israel had a special covenant with God. The blessings held out to Israel show not only the Fathers desire to bless, but also the many areas in which He desires to bless:

"And all these blessings shall come upon you and overtake you, because you obey the voice of the LORD your God: Blessed shall you be in the city, and blessed shall you be in the country. Blessed shall be the fruit of your body, the produce of your ground and the increase of your herds, the increase of your cattle and the offspring of your flocks. Blessed shall be your basket and your kneading bowl. Blessed shall you be when you come in, and blessed shall you be when you go out. The LORD will cause your enemies who rise against you to be defeated before your face; they shall come out against you one way and flee before you seven ways. The LORD will command the blessing on you in your storehouses and in all to which you set your hand, and He will bless you in the land which the LORD your God is giving you. The LORD will establish you as a holy people to Himself, just as He has sworn to you, if you keep the commandments of the LORD your God and walk in His ways. Then all peoples of the earth shall see that you are called by the name of the LORD, and they shall be afraid of you. And the LORD will grant you plenty of goods, in the fruit of your body, in the increase of your livestock, and in the produce of your ground, in the land of which the LORD swore to your fathers to give you. The LORD will open to you His good treasure, the heavens, to give the rain to your land in its season, and to bless all the work of your hand. You shall lend to many nations, but you shall not borrow. And the LORD will make you the head and not the tail; you shall be above only, and not be beneath, if you heed the commandments of the LORD your God, which I command you today, and are careful to observe them. (Deut. 28:2–13)

Nevertheless I am continually with You;
You hold me by my right hand. (Ps. 73:23)

The blessing of the LORD makes one rich,
And He adds no sorrow with it. (Prov. 10:22)

For the LORD God is a sun and shield;
The LORD will give grace and glory;
No good thing will He withhold
From those that walk uprightly. (Ps. 84:11)

His descendants will be mighty on earth;
The generation of the upright will be blessed.
(Ps. 112:2)

All these promises and many more belong to every believer. When we walk in the ways of the Lord, when we live according to God's principles and meet the conditions outlined throughout the Word of God, God promises to pour out blessings to such a degree that we cannot contain them.

God's Blessings for the Children of Israel: No Lack

God's love for His children and His willingness to bless are clearly illustrated in His dealings with the children of Israel. His faithfulness to them year after year extended into every aspect of their lives. And the promises of God to the children of Israel found throughout the old covenant are extended to you and me as His children today.

The children of Israel knew supernatural provision, for they experienced no lack. Now I have chosen every word in the sentence above *very* carefully. As the nation of Israel walked in obedience to God, God met their every need, and so they never knew lack. When you and I are walking in obedience with our loving heavenly Father, we will lack for *nothing*. The Scriptures are so bold as to assert:

> For the LORD your God has blessed you in all the work of your hand. He knows your trudging through this great wilderness. These forty years the LORD your God has been with you; *you have lacked nothing.* (Deut. 2:7, emphasis added)

> And I have led you forty years in the wilderness. Your clothes have not worn out on you, and your sandals have not worn out on your feet. (Deut. 29:5)

> Forty years You sustained them in the wilderness;
> They lacked nothing;
> Their clothes did not wear out
> And their feet did not swell. (Neh. 9:21)

When we experience no lack, God is meeting our *need*, not our *greed*. Notice that the Israelites weren't provided new shoes; rather, the heavenly Father superintended over them such that the shoes they had never wore out. Our gracious Father didn't supply them with a closet full of clothes; rather, He made sure that the clothes they had lasted far beyond normal. Our loving Father didn't put His people on the Concorde to get them from Egypt to Israel; instead, He stayed by them in the wilderness and made sure that their feet didn't swell as they walked to the promised land.

Our loving heavenly Father promised to make the nation of Israel a testimony of His faithfulness to bless generation after generation:

I will make you a great nation;
I will bless you
And make your name great;
And you shall be a blessing. (Gen. 12:2)

Blessing I will bless you, and multiplying I will multiply your descendants as the stars of the heaven and as the sand which is on the seashore; and your descendants shall possess the gate of their enemies. (Gen. 22:17)

For the LORD your God will bless you just as He promised you; you shall lend to many nations, but you shall not borrow; you shall reign over many nations, but they shall not reign over you. (Deut. 15:6)

The LORD will command the blessing on you in your storehouses and in all to which you set your hand, and He will bless you in the land which the LORD your God is giving you. (Deut. 28:8)

And He will love you and bless you and multiply you; He will also bless the fruit of your womb and the fruit of your land, your grain and your new wine and your oil, the increase of your cattle and the offspring of your flock, in the land of which He swore to your fathers to give you. (Deut. 7:13)

So they shall put My name on the children of Israel, and I will bless them. (Num. 6:27)

Divine health was also included in God's promised blessings to the children of Israel: "So you shall serve the LORD your God, and He will bless your bread and your water. And I will take sickness away from the midst of you." (Ex. 23:25)

And even when the children of Israel lost sight of God's faithfulness while facing the Red Sea and the approaching Egyptian army, complaining that it would be better to die in bondage rather than in the wilderness, God was patient and long-suffering with them. He opened the Red Sea before them and delivered them from danger. And the same waters that parted before them, allowing them to walk on dry ground, later rushed in to drown their oppressors, the Egyptians.

Time after time God demonstrated His goodness toward them in the wilderness by meeting their need, even though they grumbled and complained. Morning after morning as they awakened, they found fresh food—manna—on the ground. All they had to do was gather it. And as they ate the fresh manna, they were reminded that God brought them out of Egypt.

At one point the children of Israel complained about their hardships when they had no water, saying to Moses, "Why did you bring us out of Egypt anyway? Everything wasn't perfect there, but at least we had water to drink!"

When Moses cried out to God for help with the grumbling of the people, God directed him to strike a rock with his stick. When he did, a stream of fresh, clear water burst forth, and there was enough water for every person and every animal. Once again God demonstrated that He was with them. Just as He had always promised, there would be no lack. Our heavenly Father in His wisdom did not give them Perrier, but He met their need for water.

Even after the disgraceful incident of idolatry with the golden calf, our merciful heavenly Father was still long-suffering with the children of Israel. Moses admonished them to beg for God's forgiveness while he went back to the place where he had met God. There he pleaded with God for mercy for the people. And after forty days he returned, visibly radiant with the presence of God.

Throughout the forty-year-long journey through the wilderness, the children of Israel had no lack because God provided for them. He delivered them from their enemies, from sickness, and from peril. He was faithful to every promise He made to them.

God's faithfulness to His promises continues today. There is no expiration date on His timeless promises to bless His children.

Just in Time So many times we can be perplexed and even discouraged when our heavenly Father doesn't answer our prayers according to our timetable. We pray for God to intervene, but He doesn't seem to. We pray for a loved one to surrender to the Lord Jesus, but the person keeps living in rebellion. We pray for a financial need to be met, but nothing happens.

Years ago I heard Corrie Ten Boom share a powerful illustration about the timeliness of God's loving care. The setting for the story was Nazi-occupied Holland where she and her family were experiencing trials while attempting to shelter Jews. In the midst of increasing danger and turmoil she said, "Papa, everything is getting too bad. If the police come for us, how will we know that God is with us?"

"Corrie," he responded, "when we go on a trip by train, when do I give you the ticket?"

"Just before we get on the train, Papa," Corrie answered.

"That's right, Corrie," her father said. "You don't need your ticket until you are about to board the train. But I always give you your ticket just in time. That's how our wonderful heavenly Father is. He always gives us just what we need, and He is never late. His love and mercy will sustain us and strengthen us just when we need them, for He is always faithful."

D. L. Moody was a giant in the history of the church, a man who knew God and experienced His love and blessings continually. A friend told a story that I found fascinating, one that I would like to share with you.

It seems that in 1893, D. L. Moody had a financial need of $3,000. Mr. Moody always took his needs to the Lord in prayer, and this day was no different.

He knelt down beside his desk and prayed, "Lord, You know I need $3,000 today. I must have it, and You know that I am too busy with Your work to go out and get it. Please send it to me. I thank You that You will. Amen."

Following his prayer, Mr. Moody rose to his feet and went on about his work at the Bible Institute in Chicago.

Later that day he was scheduled to preach in the auditorium. The audience was in place, and the platform was filled with people. As the meeting was about to begin, a young woman walked up to an usher and said, "I must see Mr. Moody." He responded, "You can't see Mr. Moody now. The meeting is about to begin."

She continued, "But I must see Mr. Moody."

Unmoved by her persistence, the usher turned her away.

As she walked away, she noticed another aisle and approached another usher, making the same request to see Mr. Moody. He, too, said that would be impossible because the meeting was about to begin.

Determined, she went around to the platform entrance

and somehow found her way to where Mr. Moody stood. She put an envelope in Mr. Moody's hand when he brushed past her, making his way to the platform. As he walked onto the stage, he hastily put the envelope into his vest pocket and went on with the meeting.

Later that evening as he ate his dinner, he remembered the envelope. He reached into his vest pocket and took out the envelope. When he opened it, he discovered that it contained a check for $3,000—an answer to his prayer.

He eventually learned the story behind the heaven-sent gift. That morning the Lord had touched the heart of a Christian woman as Mr. Moody came to mind: "These are very busy days for Mr. Moody. He must need a great deal of money." And with that she made out a check for $1,000. As soon as she had written the check, the Holy Spirit spoke to her and said, "That will not be sufficient. He will need more money than that."

Obedient to the Spirit's prompting, she tore up the check and made out a new check in the amount of $2,000. Once again she was prompted by the Spirit that the amount was not adequate. She tore up the second check and proceeded to write a check for $3,000. She put the check in an envelope, sealed the envelope, addressed it, and asked her maid to mail the envelope for her. Just as the maid was about to leave the room, the woman called out to her and said, "Just a moment. He may not get it until tomorrow, and he may need it today. Put your coat on and go over to the auditorium. Give it to Mr. Moody, and do not let anyone else have it."

You see, good fathers know the needs of their children and take care of them, and children who experience the warmth of that love trust the goodness of their fathers implicitly. Just as D. L. Moody trusted his all-sufficient heavenly Father to lovingly provide for him, so we can apply the same principles. God's disposition toward His children has not changed one iota. His promises are timeless and extended to all, and He earnestly desires to bless us and provide for every area of need. The Word of God tells us, "And all these blessings shall come on thee, and overtake thee, if thou shalt hearken unto the voice of the LORD thy God." (Deut. 28:2 KJV)

My friend, I know that like me, you want the great blessing that comes from a love relationship with our heavenly Father to be visited upon your life. The Bible contains very clear guidelines on how we can experience the blessings promised to God's children—and I want so much for you to understand them and make them a reality in your life. Are you ready to apply these principles and begin your journey on the biblical road to blessing?

CHAPTER

3

A Journey to the Father's Love

Getting Acquainted

"Have a seat, Benny," the gentleman said, ushering me into his family room. "Let's get comfortable and have a talk."

I moved quickly in the direction the man was pointing and took a seat. Although I had known the man in a professional capacity for some time, we were about to become acquainted on a personal basis. The reason: I was about to become his son-in-law.

The man was Rev. Roy Harthern, a pastor whose pulpit I had filled as an evangelist on several occasions, and the father of Suzanne, the woman I had chosen to marry.

As we sat facing each other in his family room, Suzanne's father said, "Tell me about yourself."

I said, "Fine, what would you like to know?" and settled in for what I anticipated would be a very pleasant get-acquainted conversation. After all, I wanted to marry his daughter, and it seemed quite fair that he should know who I was.

"Tell me about yourself, Benny," Roy said.

I thought he must be curious about my family and my background so I prepared to tell him all about myself. I went through my whole history, including everything that seemed important. I even told him about moving from

Israel to Toronto which he already knew, but I didn't want to leave anything out. After all, this man was to be my father-in-law soon.

Roy asked me questions about this and that, and as I answered each question, I thought, *He really wants to know everything about who his girl is going to marry.* Up to that time he had known me as an evangelist because I had spoken at his church on a couple of occasions. God had moved powerfully in those meetings, and I felt blessed to be a part of them. We had also attended the same ministers' conference in Singapore and ended up on the same long flight home. However, our relationship was basically on a professional level, and that was about all.

I was a young evangelist with increasing opportunities for ministry. My ministry did have some bills, but I had already decided not to mention them to Roy during our chat because I didn't want him to have any undue concerns about my marrying his daughter. What I didn't know was that somehow Roy was already aware of the indebtedness.

Our conversation was relaxed and casual for several minutes. I was just beginning to get comfortable when our conversation took on a more intense tone. He asked, "Benny, do you tithe?"

Although I had been in the ministry since 1974, I really didn't understand a great deal about the subject of tithing. Although I had spent hundreds and hundreds of hours studying God's Word, I hadn't put together the teachings of the Word of God on the whole subject of giving. It was 1978, and I had never heard any strong teaching about God's principles of tithing and giving. I basically associated the word *tithing* with giving a monetary donation of some arbitrary amount . . . whatever seemed appropriate at the time. So, every time I went to church, I gave something . . . whatever seemed right at the time.

Somewhat stunned by his question, however, I cleared

my throat and responded slowly, "Well, Roy . . . ah . . . that's between God and me."

Roy looked me straight in the eyes and said, "You're about to become my son-in-law. I promise it'll be between God, you, and *me*."

Startled by his direct follow-up statement, I paused for a moment. His question made me a bit nervous, and I wasn't quite sure how to answer. "Well . . . you see, Roy . . . it's like this . . ." My words trailed off as I searched for an intelligent, appropriate response. I was getting more nervous by the minute. As I tried to think of what I should say, my mind was filled with thoughts like, *Why is this man asking me this? What has this got to do with marriage anyway? This is none of his business!*

"Well," I continued slowly, trying to sound confident, "you know, sometimes I give this much money and then at other times I give that much money to God," mentioning specific amounts I had given in the past. "Actually, I guess you could say that I give what I feel like giving."

He sat up abruptly, pointed his finger in my face, and said emphatically, "Now I know!"

"Now you know what?" I inquired.

"I have been sitting here racking my brain wondering why a successful young evangelist like you is in debt. You ought to have money in the bank. And here you are in debt. Now I know."

"Please tell me," I responded, "because I'd like to know why I'm in debt too."

"Because you are an emotional giver!" Roy said decidedly.

"What are you talking about?" I asked, trying very hard not to allow my voice to betray the irritation I felt. First he asked me a question that really was none of his business, and then he told me that I was an emotional giver. About that time I was thinking, *This man is going to be my father-in-law? Forget it.*

Roy responded quickly, "You just told me that sometimes you give this much and sometimes you give that
much," repeating the amounts I had just mentioned. "You
give more when you feel good, and you give less when you
don't! You give more when the preacher blesses you, and
when he doesn't, you give less. If you have a good morning,
you give more; if you have a bad morning, you give less.
That's emotional giving. How would you like God to give
back to you in the way you've been giving to Him?"

I said, "He does! Sometimes the offerings are big and
sometimes they're not! Sometimes it's good and sometimes
it's bad!"

Roy leaned forward and said, "Never forget this, Benny.
The law of giving is a fixed law you cannot change. Emotional giving is cursed by God." As he spoke, I could feel the
anointing on the words he was sharing.

"So what do I do, Roy?" I asked. "I'm in such debt."

"I'll tell you how to get out of debt," Roy said.

"Please, I'm listening," I responded, eager to hear what
he was about to say.

"Start paying God's bills," Roy said decisively.

"Roy, I don't have enough money to pay *my* bills," I
answered.

Roy practically ignored my statement and continued,
"Benny, if you'll pay God's bills, He'll pay yours. The Word
of God says the law of giving is a fixed law. You cannot
change it nor can you give because of emotions. You must
give because it's commanded. You give because it's the law
of God. And if you'll do that, He'll bring you out of debt.
Go back home and start paying God's bills. And if you'll do
that, He'll bring you out of debt."

No one had ever talked to me about giving, nor had
anyone ever had the boldness to talk to me in this way before.

"What do I do now?" I asked, desperate for answers.

"Well, you do two things," Roy continued. "Number

one, you begin giving now, and number two, you pay back everything you owe God.''

I must have been staring at Roy as I inquired, "What did you say?''

"The Old Testament says that if you miss giving your tithes, you must pay back what you missed giving and add 20 percent on top of what you owe.''

Amazed, I exclaimed, "I owe God more money than I owe my creditors!''

"You're right, Benny,'' Roy said.

"Are you telling me that I am in debt more than I thought?'' I asked.

Roy repeated, "The Word of God says if you miss tithing and giving, you must pay that back with 20 percent over.''

"In that case, I'm hundreds of thousands of dollars in debt!'' I declared. "What do I do?''

"You start paying God's bills, and He'll pay yours,'' Roy again stated emphatically.

Decisions, Decisions

As I flew back to my home in Toronto, Roy's words kept coming back to me: "If you'll pay God's bills, He'll pay yours.'' I knew God had spoken to me and I knew Roy was right, but I was going through a battle during the entire flight. I wanted to obey God, but the circumstances I was facing were causing such a struggle in my mind. "Dear Lord Jesus,'' I prayed, "whom do I obey? I know Roy is right, but what do I do about all those bills?''

And did I have bills! I was living in Toronto, Canada, and had been ministering for about four years. The Lord began blessing the ministry greatly, and things began to grow and expand. I began holding Monday night services in a big Anglican church that seated approximately 3,600 people and later moved to a different building.

With everything going so well, two men had advised me to go on television. They said, "Oh, look at this. The Lord is using you, you have the crowds, and you're doing great. Why not go on television?"

Accepting their advice, I said, "Okay, that's a good idea."

We began a weekly program called "It's a Miracle" on a secular Canadian television station in 1977. The program was on each Sunday at 10:00 P.M. right after "60 Minutes." It was a desirable time slot on a good station, but the problem was that my going on television was man's idea—not God's. God had never told me to go on television.

According to the contract for the television program, the program would air each Sunday evening for twenty eight weeks. In the contract I also agreed to tape the programs in the facilities at the station. Consequently, with the cost of the studio time to prepare the programs and the weekly air time, I was in debt overnight. I had never been in debt in my life, but suddenly, I was in debt up to my neck. I paid my bills each week, only to discover that when I arrived at the office on Monday, I had more bills to pay: some that I didn't even know about.

The financial pressures related to the television program and production costs began to affect my services. Before long my freedom to minister was hindered by the bondage that the debt brought to my life. Soon the offerings were not sufficient to pay the bills. I was forced to take two offerings: one for the ministry and one for television.

One bad decision led to another. At about the same time I had planned a Holy Land trip, but because of finances, I was forced to cancel the trip. The travel agency initiated legal action for canceling the trip. So I was faced with the problem and debt all at the same time. I was thinking, *Lord, what did I do wrong?* I was asking in sincerity, not realizing that what I had done wrong was listening to men and thinking God was in their plan. That's why it is so important to know the will of God.

And to make matters worse, I had fallen in love and was

making plans to get married. It had all happened so suddenly, and I discovered that falling in love can be very expensive.

Divine Appointment   Let me briefly share what happened. I was traveling in those days and ministering. At about that time, I met Ronn Haus, who is now my associate evangelist. Ronn introduced me to Roy Harthern, who at that time had the largest Assembly of God church in the nation. It was located in Orlando, Florida, and Calvary Assembly had an attendance of ten thousand people every week. Roy invited me to preach for him. I accepted, and we had five services that Sunday. The anointing of the Lord was powerful in those services.

I was invited back to Calvary, and I accepted. Not long after preaching at Calvary, I was on my way to Singapore for a David du Plessis conference. Ronn Haus was working with David du Plessis, and I was looking forward to seeing him at the conference. My flight ended up being canceled, and I had to be rerouted through Thailand. That made the trip much longer, and I barely arrived before the conference had ended.

My schedule made it necessary to return to Toronto almost immediately. I was frustrated that my travel problems had kept me from attending most of the conference. When I boarded the plane to return home, however, I discovered that Roy Harthern was on the flight. We ended up sitting together for the entire flight. At one point, Roy got out his wallet and said, "I want to show you my girls." Although I had already preached for him twice, I hadn't met Suzanne because she was attending Evangel College, an Assemblies of God college in Springfield, Missouri.

He showed me the pictures of his three daughters, one by one, telling me their names. As he held out the photo of his daughter, Suzanne, the Lord spoke to me and said, "She is going to be your wife." He did not speak to me in an audible voice, but I knew that the Lord was speaking to me in that moment nonetheless.

"Lord," I said, "this is not the time to tell me about a wife. I'm in debt." Later I discovered that the Lord had told Roy the same thing on that plane, but he didn't tell me what God had said, and I certainly didn't mention it to him.

Not long after that, Roy invited me to be a guest at his home for Christmas. I accepted and made plans to be there during the holidays. Suzanne came home from college to celebrate Christmas with her family. However, when I arrived, Suzanne had gone to a friend's house.

I learned later that Suzanne had left for her friend's house because she was very nervous about the prospect of meeting me. Anyway, Roy, his wife Pauline, and I went over to the friend's house to pick up Suzanne for dinner. The moment I saw her I had a funny feeling in my knees. I heard the Lord speak the same words to me, "She is going to be your wife."

I said, "Lord, this is not the time to tell me about a wife. I've got bills to pay . . . I'm in financial trouble, Lord." And even though I was arguing with God, I felt a tugging deep within, and I knew that God was speaking to me.

Almost Home

As my flight to Toronto continued and the airplane got closer and closer to home, Roy's words kept ringing in my ears: "If you'll pay God's bills, He'll pay yours." This phrase kept playing over and over in my mind. Deep within I knew he was right. Just before the plane landed in Toronto, I finally came to a decision. I would obey God!

It was Wednesday, and the airport was only about ten minutes from my office. I was on the ground by noon and headed straight for the office. I greeted my secretary and said, "Marian, get the checkbook out."

"What for?" she inquired.

"Just get it out," I repeated.

"Okay," she said as she went to her desk to retrieve the ministry checkbook.

"Send a check for $1,000 to . . . ," and with that I directed her to send specific amounts to a number of ministers and ministries. Her hand began to shake as she wrote the checks. After a check or two, she paused and asked, "What are you doing?"

"I'm just obeying God," I said.

"Are you sure God is talking to you?" she asked.

"Absolutely!" I announced.

"What do you want me to do?" she inquired.

"Send $1,000 to . . . and $1,000 to. . . . "On and on the list went.

Suddenly, the poor woman said, "Wait, wait. You're going to be out of money soon and go bankrupt." She paused and looked down at the list. Then she looked up at me and said, "What are you doing? These are not people to whom you owe any money."

"I know," I responded. "That's money I owe God, so let's obey Him!"

Once I had won my battle on the airplane, I had begun to calculate just how much I owed God. I was born again in 1972, and it was 1978. As I added all the years I had neglected to tithe, I realized that I owed God more than I owed the television station. And I was determined to begin obeying God.

With my list concluded, my secretary finished writing out the checks. As she filled in the amounts, her hand was trembling. In fact, when she realized that nearly the entire balance of the account would be needed to cover all the checks, she got so nervous that she called all my board members. All nine came to the office within the hour and asked, "What are you doing?"

I said, "I'm obeying God!"

"But you're in debt. You can't do that," they protested. "We have bills to pay."

"I'm obeying God. I'm paying God's bills," I said firmly.

My CPA spoke up and said, "Benny, you're going to go bankrupt. You don't even have the money to pay your own bills. What are you doing, giving all the money away?"

"You don't understand," I said with determination. "I must obey God!"

"But you owe the television station and you owe . . . ," and with that my board members began listing the names of my creditors.

"Look," I said, "God told me through a man to pay Him first."

Bewildered, my CPA resigned. Then my lawyer resigned. Another board member followed his lead and said, "I'm sorry. I don't want to be a part of a bankrupt ministry!" One by one, seven of the nine board members resigned. Everyone resigned except two men.

As my two remaining board members stood there with my secretary and me, Fred Brown said with his lips trembling, "Are you sure God spoke to you?"

"Yes," I said confidently and without hesitation.

"Weeelll, if God spoke to you, I'll stick with you," he said.

"Thank you," I said.

"Me too," responded Fred Spring, who is now on my staff and has been for many years.

The sum of all those checks emptied the account. And poor Marian, her face was pale white as she closed the checkbook and we all went home.

That was Wednesday. On Thursday and Friday I didn't go to the office. With an empty checking account, there was nothing left to send to any of the creditors, and I didn't want to be there to answer the telephone. I knew that I had nothing to lose. I was in debt in the natural, but I knew that it was more important to obey God. Trusting God, I cleaned out that bank account. I said, "Lord, if Roy's right and you said, 'Prove me now herewith . . . if I will not open you the windows of heaven, and pour you out a blessing, that there shall not be room enough to receive it.' (Mal, 3:10 KJV), I'm proving You, Lord. I'm proving You without a thing left in the account."

A Dime in My Pocket

The following Sunday I went to church. In those days I drove an old white two-door Pontiac with a red roof, a car that had at one time belonged to my younger brother, Willie. I made it to church, even though I hardly had enough gas in the car to get there and back home again. I walked into church with only one dime in my pocket. That was all the money I had, but it was the first Sunday that I was actually going to tithe. I was thinking, *ten cents . . . so that means I must give God one cent.*"

As the minister prepared to receive the offering and the ushers distributed the offering buckets, I realized I didn't have one cent to give. I had only a dime. So as the offering bucket came by, even though I really wanted to give the tithe on the ten cents I had in my pocket, I didn't put in anything because I didn't have any change.

As I held the offering bucket in my hand, I heard the Lord say, "Give it."

Lord, You can't be serious, I thought. *I just gave all the money in the bank account, and now it's gone.*

"No, you didn't give it all. There is another ten cents in your pocket," He said. "Give it."

The conviction of the Spirit of God was so strong that I began to perspire. I fought over that ten cents more than I fought over the thousands in the account. I thought, *I can't believe God would ask this of me.*

Then the Lord spoke to me once again and said, "I want you to give this ten cents sacrificially. It's the key that will unlock heaven for you."

Slowly, I reached into my pocket and pulled out my last dime. I sat there staring at the dime in my hand for a moment. I struggled with the thought of giving it because it was all I had. I finally placed it in the offering bucket. The hardest thing to do that morning was to give that ten cents away. Although I could have done very little with only ten cents, I think it was more difficult for me to give that dime than it had been to give away all the money in the ministry account the previous Wednesday.

Monday Morning's Mail

I woke up early Monday morning and prepared to start my day. I thought, *Lord, what do I do now? The bank account is empty, my money is all gone, I have no personal money in the bank, and I still owe You more than I owe anyone else.*

I was nervous as I got ready to go to the office. I had to borrow money from my brother to put gas in the car just to get there. Shortly after I arrived, one of my two board members dropped by just to make sure that I was okay. Not long after he came by, the mail arrived, and I thought, *Ohhh, Lord, more bills! Ohhh, what do I do now?*

My poor secretary, Marian, was sick that morning. She looked pale, but she came in anyway because we knew that it was going to be the week of decision.

I opened the first envelope. I was shocked. It was from one of the individuals I had directed my secretary to prepare a check for the previous Wednesday. I couldn't believe my eyes at first because he wasn't particularly fond of me and told me so himself. There was a check for $1,000. He included a note that said, "The Lord woke me up Wednesday night and told me to send you this." He sent that check before he received mine. I was thinking, *Boy, it must be real. It must be God.*

I said, "Dear Jesus, Roy is right! But it's only $1,000, and I've got a long way to go." The moment I saw the amount of the check, the Lord spoke clearly and said, "Tell your secretary to write out a check for $100 right now. Don't wait!

Send that to . . . ." And I mailed that $100 off that same day.

I continued opening the mail, one envelope at a time, and by the time Friday arrived, $8,000. had come in from people who said, "God told me to send you this." God spoke; God spoke; God spoke; God spoke. God did not move on my behalf until I obeyed Him. I had discovered a marvelous truth: whatever moves you moves God! Whatever moves you will move heaven on your behalf!

Money began coming in miraculously. People began writing me unexpectedly—even some who had never expressed any real warmth or friendship toward me—and within a few months I was totally out of debt.

Principles to Live By

That was 1978.

And through those events, I discovered so much more about our wonderful Lord and His love for us. Since the moment I first met Him and surrendered my heart and life to Him in 1972, I have known a dimension of love that I never experienced elsewhere. The love of my heavenly Father was so fresh and real, so gentle and caring—much different from anything I ever knew in the natural. You see, my relationship with my father was not like that.

My father was a big man who was very stern. I loved my father, but as a child, I was uncertain of my relationship with him. The gnawing question of whether or not my father loved me plagued me constantly. I don't recall ever hearing him say while I was growing up, "I love you, Benny." Rather than show the warmth and emotion of a father to his children, he functioned more as the commanding officer of a military organization. He issued the orders, and we children were expected to obey with no questions or discussion. I tried to please him by being obedient and by being a good student, but my efforts seemed to go unnoticed. How I longed for his love and acceptance, and how precious were the days after he came to know the Lord when God opened his heart and allowed him to express the love that he felt toward me all of those years!

Imagine how I felt when I began to experience the warmth of my heavenly Father's love. Never had I known such unconditional acceptance. That drew me to spend time in His presence, day after day.

It was as if I was a man who had been lost in the desert for days with only a few ounces of water, but suddenly came upon a cool, crystal river of fresh water. Just a sip of that water after days in a parched desert would not be adequate to satisfy the unquenchable thirst. The love and acceptance that I felt were much like cool, clear water in the middle of the desert, so pure and fresh, and so available without limitation. Never before had I been accepted just as I was. But the love that I felt from my heavenly Father was unlike anything I had ever known. It was wonderful!

When I came to that well of salvation in 1972, my unquenchable thirst was satisfied as it had never been before. I was transformed by God's love in a moment's time and accepted just as I was. Not long afterward I was introduced to the person of the Holy Spirit, who became my companion and friend as I have shared in my books *Good Morning, Holy Spirit* and *Welcome, Holy Spirit.*

Law vs. Love

The Holy Spirit used Roy to teach me about the subject of giving and tithing, and challenged me to begin giving from a biblical perspective. Although Roy helped me in a tremendous way to understand the biblical principles of giving that brought blessings to my life and ministry, I saw it more as my obligation or a matter of law. I didn't fully understand that God wants to bless His children abundantly because of His boundless love for us.

I didn't really become aware of God's care for finances in our lives until the mid-eighties. And it happened while I was watching an interview with Dr. W. A. Criswell, a pastor, leader, and respected man of God in the Southern Baptist Convention. And here, too, the Holy Spirit was still teaching me.

I'll never forget it. Here was a great man who pastored the largest Southern Baptist church in America, and had served as president of the Southern Baptist Convention two times (which is the maximum allowed). He was viewed as a statesman in the Baptist community, and he had a strong following on both television and radio. And as I heard Dr. Criswell talk about how much God wants His children blessed, I was totally captivated by what he was saying. He spoke with such conviction, and there was an underlying element of love in everything he said about giving. His words brought new meaning to the whole subject.

Giving from a Heart of Love

What he was saying was in the Bible, and it was life to me! He presented a picture of giving as an act of worship and love—not just a responsibility or duty. I had been giving, but without really having the deep, settled knowledge of God's love for me. Dr. Criswell's teaching on giving helped me understand that giving was an expression and extension of my worship—just because I loved the Lord.

It's like this: in the Old Testament, God sent Moses to the children of Israel to show Israel His mind. As the messenger of God, Moses delivered the Ten Commandments to the children of Israel, representing the laws by which they should live.

In the New Testament, God sent Jesus Christ, His only Son, to the children of Israel to reveal His heart to them. Jesus Christ was God's messenger, but the message was one of love and relationship.

What I had learned initially from Roy could be compared with the law that Moses delivered to Israel. Although it was for their good, it was lacking in relationship and was established more on legalism. What I learned through Dr. Criswell's interview that day was that giving can be an expression of our love and worship to the Lord. When it became an act of worship, it was so much easier for me to give out of a heart of love.

I had a new interest and desire to study God's Word to find out all I could on the subject of giving and God's blessings. God had given me so much by sending His only begotten Son, Jesus Christ. I began to ask questions, such as, "What do You want me to give, Lord? What can I give back to express my love for You?" With Dr. Criswell's words, the tithe began to take on new meaning as a description of God's care.

I had been tithing, but I had been doing so out of a sense of duty or responsibility, and at times perhaps out of fear of what would happen if I didn't give. I heard Dr. Criswell say that he has come to feel that God cares for each of us and wants to bless us as His children beyond our ability to receive it, but He is unable to do so without our obedience. All God is looking for is our obedient love.

Dr. Criswell helped me understand that God doesn't just care about our obeying the law. Rather, He cares more about His children obeying the law because we love Him. For after all, the very first commandment is, "Thou shalt love the LORD thy God with all thine heart, and with all thy soul, and with all thy might." (Deut. 6:5 KJV) And the entire law is based on loving God.

The teaching became life to me and changed my entire perspective on giving. I had not been excited about giving before because I felt obligated. But when I understood more fully how giving can be an expression of my love and gratitude to God, I became the cheerful giver that God's Word urges us to become: "God loves a cheerful giver." (2 Cor. 9:7b) I was first a giver—now I have become a *cheerful* giver. We cannot give cheerfully without the knowledge of the love of God.

He won me to giving with His love. Giving was no longer a battle for me, for I understood that I could give out of obedience, and that obedience was based on loving God supremely rather than fearing His law. I was giving because of relationship.

As a child, I always obeyed my father because he was my father. That type of obedience is based more on law. But I obey my heavenly Father because He is my Father and I love Him.

People who give because they are taught to give are not yet won by God's Spirit, and they will not have the results. But when we give because we love and adore Him, giving becomes as normal and natural as breathing. It's no longer forced or thought about; no battle takes place. When we give out of a heart of love, there is no other reason than our love for Him. A glorious transformation takes place when giving becomes an act of worship.

Dr. Criswell helped me understand that when you love, you don't care if you lose. Job was a lover of God, and nothing could affect the way he felt about God. Job said, "The LORD gave and the LORD hath taken away; blessed be the name of the LORD." (Job 1:21 KJV) Even after he had lost his possessions and his children, his love for God was still unchanged, for he said, "Though he slay me, yet will I trust in him." (Job 13:15 KJV)

Works or Relationship?

Many people attempt to obligate God through their works. But this is not what moves God, for God looks on the heart.

I can remember hearing a story about my uncle's father-in-law in Jaffa. He was a very religious man who thought his works could obligate God to answer his prayers for more children.

He decided that the only way he could get what he wanted was to prove to God that he was really religious. He decided to demonstrate his devotion to God by going from his house to the church *on his knees.* When he finally arrived at the church after his painful journey, his knees were bloody and bruised. Certain that heaven had been moved by his demonstration of devotion and religion, he made his request to God.

He waited and waited, but no answer came. He eventually became a hard-hearted atheist whose heart was filled with hatred until the day he died. He died never realizing that God was looking not for an outward demonstration of the flesh, but for an inward commitment of the heart.

When the three Hebrew children were about to be thrown into the fiery furnace after refusing to worship the golden image, their love for God and faith in Him were strong and unwavering. They said, "Our God whom we serve is able to deliver us from the burning fiery furnace, and He will deliver us from your hand, O king. But if not, let it be known to you, O king, that we do not serve your gods, nor will we worship the gold image which you have set up." (Dan. 3:17) Their love was sacrificial in that they stood firm in their faith. They wouldn't bend, they wouldn't bow, *and they didn't burn!*

Growing and Learning

Since I saw that marvelous interview with Dr. Criswell, I have learned so much about God's principles of giving through tithes and offerings. I have found that no matter how hard I try, I cannot out give God. The more I give to the Master, the more He gives to me, so I can give again.

As R. T. Kendall, a perceptive writer on the topic of biblical giving, said, "Honor Him with your substance and you will see Him work in a manner that will exceed your greatest expectations."[1]

I have discovered that you can stake your life on the principles of tithing and giving recorded in God's Word. God's law of giving is a fixed law that you cannot change—

just as His love *never* wavers. The "give and it shall be given unto you" of the gospel is true.

The following pages contain much of what I have learned over the years about God's principles of tithing and giving, both from a study of God's Word and from personal experience. Since that day in 1978 when I made a decision to honor God in my giving and began to tithe, great blessings have come upon my life, my ministry, my family, and my walk with God. Some mistakenly connect blessings to finances, but that is only one area of life in which God blesses. The blessings I have experienced in my ministry and in my walk with God are beyond anything I ever dreamed possible. And as I have faithfully honored God in my giving, my finances have also been blessed, enabling me to give more to the work of the Lord so that the message of His glorious gospel might be proclaimed to the ends of the earth.

Muller and Money

George Muller was a young German Christian who lived in England in the early 1800s and loved God with every atom of his being. That man of God discovered what can be accomplished through an ordinary man who trusts in an extraordinary God. His unwavering, childlike dependence upon his heavenly Father for every need and God's faithfulness to provide gave him a perspective on finances that is simple but profound.

In his autobiography he said:

Money is of no value to me unless I can use it for God. The more I pay out for the work of God, the more prospect I have of being further supplied by Him. The larger the sum I obtain from Him, in answer to prayer, the greater is the proof of the blessedness and the reality of dealing directly with God alone for what I need. Therefore, I have as much joy in giving as in receiving.[2]

Many believers have never experienced the joy and fulfillment that come as a result of giving to the Lord's work in tithes and offerings. They have never known the satisfaction of honoring God through their giving. As a result, they have also never known the blessings that can come upon every area of their lives as a result of that obedience.

Love, the Basis for Relationship

When we love someone, it is easy to share what we have and who we are. The same principle holds true with our heavenly Father.

Scripture often referred to David as a man after God's own heart. Although he was not perfect, he loved God and fellowshipped with Him. And in Psalm 51:16–17 (KJV), we find that David had discovered the secret to a relationship with God: "For thou desirest not sacrifice; else would I give it: thou delightest not in burnt offering. The sacrifices of God are a broken spirit: a broken and a contrite heart, O God, thou wilt not despise." He had discovered the two sacrifices that are always acceptable: (1) a broken spirit and (2) a broken and contrite heart.

God doesn't want fleshly, forced obedience. Rather, He is looking for loving obedience. Do I see Him as a rigid, mean boss, ready to whip me for every mistake I make? No, He is not like that. He is a tenderhearted heavenly Father, full of mercy and grace. David said, "Your lovingkindness is better than life." (Ps. 63:3a) David had discovered the basis for true riches, and as a result of his relationship with God, he was abundantly blessed.

Through the Eyes of Others

God uses different people to show different aspects of His love. His love for me in connection with the giving of the Holy Spirit was revealed through the life and ministry of Kathryn Kuhlman. God used her in a wonderful way, and the Holy Spirit touched my heart through her life.

Through her ministry, I began to realize that God loved me so much, He wanted me to have His anointing on my life. Not only did He desire that for me, but it was available to me.

Just as God used Kathryn Kuhlman to bring great understanding to my life regarding the anointing of the Holy Spirit, He chose to use my father-in-law, Roy Harthern, and Dr. W. A. Criswell to show me that He wanted to bless me financially. And through them, I have come to understand that God's love for me is directly related to His intense desire to bring financial blessing to my life so that I will know no lack.

When we love God in response to His love for us, everything changes. Giving is only one expression of my love for Him. I love him in my service, in my worship, in my dedication, in my life, in my obedience. Everything I do must be an expression of that love. If my love for Him is not evident in everything I do, then I don't really love Him.

In Mark 12:30 we read, "And you shall love the LORD your God with all your heart, and with all your soul, with all your mind, and with all your strength."

To love God with all your heart means with every atom of your being. He wants you to love Him supremely and with everything that is within you.

When you are commanded to love God with all your soul, you are to love Him with all your emotions and your intellectual will. He wants everything in your emotions and intellect to love Him.

When you love God with all your mind, you love Him with everything you understand about Him. This understanding is communicated to others as you talk about Him and introduce Him to others that they might know Him too.

When you love Him with all your strength, you love God with everything about you physically as well as in your service to Him and in your daily walk. God the Father is really saying, "I want everything about you physically to love Me:

your running, your doing, your service, what you put your body through."

The moment we have this revelation of His love we are overwhelmed by the dimension of such love that everything we are and have becomes His. Do you remember what Paul said? He said, "For the love of Christ *constraineth* us." (2 Cor. 5:14 KJV, emphasis added) In other words, "I am so moved, touched, and overwhelmed by it." Therefore, if I give God my money but my heart isn't in it, I am not expressing my love for Him with all my heart, with all my soul, with all my mind, and with all my strength. And if God is not supreme, He is not God at all.

The Joy of Giving The churches of Macedonia knew the joy of giving because they had been touched by God's love. Although they were desperately poor and persecuted, they gave generously of what they had to their impoverished and persecuted brothers and sisters in Judea.

Paul wrote, "That in a great trial of affliction the abundance of their joy and their deep poverty abounded in the riches of their liberality." (2 Cor. 8:2) Their overflowing joy welled up in the midst of "the most severe trial" and their "extreme poverty" (NIV), and they still gave. They did not hesitate, but shared freely of what they had. It was not a matter of "let me see if I can spare something." They gave because of love. Remember, "it is possible to give without loving, but we cannot love without giving. The greatest proof of this is Christ's great act of love."[3]

The moment you and I realize that God loves us, and we are touched by a revelation of His eternal love that reaches beyond time, the Holy Spirit begins to minister to us and *everything* we do becomes an expression of our love for God.

And I know that like me, you want to experience this joy and fulfillment. The information in this book is not based upon my theories or opinions. It is based upon God's Word.

It is my prayer that the eternal truths from God's Word contained within the pages of this book will bring greater understanding in the area of tithing and giving to each reader. *The truth that we know* brings liberty and sets us free. As you study and apply these principles to your life, you will learn how you, too, can experience the true joy of giving to God and the blessings that come as a result of applying these principles.

CHAPTER

4

Surrender to the Father's Love

My friend, I am more convinced than ever before that God the Father wants to bless His obedient children far more than we can handle, far more than we can even comprehend. The apostle Paul barely hinted at this when he declared:

> Eye has not seen, nor ear heard,
> Nor have entered into the heart of man
> The things which God has prepared *for those who love Him.*" (1 Cor. 2:9, emphasis added)

In some ways this verse is the key: God has prepared so much *for those who love Him.*

Experiencing the incredible life of blessing that God has for you really isn't any more complicated than falling in love with the Almighty, and so letting Him do all for you that He intends. The life of blessing He intends for you isn't found in formulas and techniques. It isn't letting go or hanging on—it's falling in love with God the Father. And as in any relationship between a good father and an obedient child, the father pours the best into the life of that child— and the child moves in love and trust with the father.

So before we explore the wonders on the biblical road

to blessing, we must begin at the beginning. And that place of beginning is *surrender*. Surrender is giving all to God without reservation. It is giving *every* part of *every* area of our lives *totally* to God *without reservation*. Many believers never experience the full measure of the bounty and blessing that the Lord intends for them because they have never fully surrendered to God.

But surrender is only part of it. The Lord doesn't want surrender just for the sake of surrender. He doesn't want us to surrender *in order* to be blessed—much less get rich. Nor does He want us to surrender out of fear of the consequences. No! He wants us to surrender because we love Him so much, we want above all to bring pleasure to Him. As any parent knows, what brings the most joy to the heart is when a child obeys simply to bring delight to the heart of the parent.

Frankly, this is another area where too many believers miss the full joy of the Christian life. Instead of falling in love with the Father and making it their aim to please the One they love, they instead obey simply because they want to receive a reward—as if any father would be pleased by this. No love is there, and it is love that pleases the Father— the kind of love that gives what is *first* and what is *best*.

Surrender, Not Leftovers

Leftovers is a word that just doesn't fit into my vocabulary, and one that I prefer to avoid on my dinner table as well! I don't enjoy them in any form.

As a young boy growing up in Israel, I always looked forward to mealtime. My mother was and still is a fabulous cook, and she spent many hours each day in the kitchen lovingly preparing the foods our family ate. Her mouth-watering delicacies were always something to look forward to. Because the majority of food products were available only as fresh produce and the like, her delicious dishes were prepared from fresh meat and vegetables.

Even the spices and seasonings she used were fresh and added so much flavor to each dish. If you walk down the streets in Israel today, you will see fresh meat and vegetables for sale in many places, and you can smell the marvelous aroma of the spices for sale too.

My mother always put so much love into her cooking, and the fragrance of whatever she was preparing filled our house. By the time the food had finished cooking, we were ready to enjoy it. And with several growing boys in the family, leftovers were never a problem. I don't like leftovers—and neither does the Lord, for He is always asking us for our best, not our leftovers.

So before we can really appreciate the Bible's principles on how God wants us to handle the resources He has blessed us with, we must first do one important thing: surrender everything to Him.

Now surrender isn't just talk. It's not a quick and cheap statement, such as, "Okay, Lord, I give You my life, but not my money"; or "I give You my love, but not my home and family." That's not surrender, because it's not a 100 percent commitment. Surrender is prayerfully saying, "Lord, You own my body, You own the work of my hands, You own my family, You own my possessions. Everything I have is Yours. You are Lord, indeed. And I want You to own my heart too." That's surrender.

Only when we have given *everything* to God for His use—not just warmed-up leftovers—will He bless and multiply to overflowing what we have placed in His hands.

Surrender is never easy, for sacrifice is required. But trust me in this, *the alternative is far more difficult.* When we look at the Master's call for sacrifice in light of how much our heavenly Father loves us, surrender is transformed from a sacrifice into a choice privilege.

As Dr. W. A. Criswell helped me understand as I watched his interview years ago, when you love, you don't care if you lose. Take Job, for example. He was a lover of

God, and nothing could affect the way he felt about God. Job said, "The LORD gave and the LORD hath taken away; blessed be the name of the LORD." (Job 1:21 KJV) Even after he had lost his possessions and his children, Job's love for God was unchanged, which is why he could say with such confidence, "Though he slay me, yet will I trust him." (Job 13:15 KJV)

When we love God in response to His love for us, *everything* changes. What and how I give back to Him are only partial expressions of my love. I also love Him in my service, in my worship, in my dedication, in my obedience, in my relationships—in everything. If my love for Him is not evident in everything I do, then I'm not totally surrendered.

In Mark 12:30 (KJV), we read, "And thou shalt love the Lord thy God with all thy heart, and with all thy soul, and with all thy mind, and with all thy strength:"

- To love God with all our *heart* means to love Him with every atom of our being.
- To love God with all our *soul* means to love Him with all our emotions and will.
- To love God with all our *mind* means to love Him with our intellect, everything we understand about Him.
- To love God with all our *strength* means to love Him with everything about us physically as well as in our service to Him.

When we grasp the dimension of His love, we are so overwhelmed that everything we are and have becomes His. As the apostle Paul declared in Galatians 2:20, "I have been crucified with Christ; it is no longer I who live, but Christ lives in me; and the life which I now live in the flesh I live by faith in the Son of God, who loved me and gave Himself for me." In the presence of such great love, we can't help being touched and overwhelmed. Truly, the love of Christ *constrains* us to give Him our very best. Our Father is never content with leftovers, for throughout Scripture, we find the Father asking for the *first* and the *best*, for *surrender*.

Surrender: Giving the First and Best

I'll never forget when I first learned from my wife, Suzanne, that she was pregnant with our firstborn, Jessica. I didn't know all that being a father meant, and to tell the truth, now that I am the father of teenagers, I'm learning all over again!

I was thirty years old when I first became a father. I can't even begin to imagine how Abraham must have felt when he learned for the first time that he would be a father—not merely of a child, but of a *great nation*. God appeared to aged Abraham and said:

> I will make you a great nation;
> I will bless you
> And make your name great;
> And you shall be a blessing.
> I will bless those who bless you,
> And I will curse him who curses you;
> And in you all the families of the earth shall be
> blessed.
> (Gen. 12:2–3)

Abraham enjoyed the blessings of God almighty in many ways: fellowship with God, a beautiful wife, vast material wealth, stunning military success, diplomatic savvy, and a long life. Yet in the midst of all of his prosperity, one blessing eluded him—he and Sarah were childless. Being in their seventies, Abraham and Sarah had doubtless long before come to grips with the idea that they would never know the joy of being parents.

Then came the amazing word from God that not only would they be parents, they would also be the founders of a great nation through whom the entire world would be blessed. And it was not exactly as if Abraham and Sarah still had the bodies of twenty-five year-olds:

> By faith Sarah herself also received strength to conceive seed, and she bore a child when she was past the age, because she judged Him faithful who had promised. Therefore from one man, *and him as good as dead*, were born as many as the stars of the sky in multitude—innumerable as the sand which is by the seashore. (Heb. 11:11–12, emphasis added)

No, the only way they would receive God's promise was through His miracle-working power.

How their hearts must have been filled with wonder at the words that the Lord spoke to them! Nor was that the only time God the Father promised them that they would experience the wonder of parenthood. He reiterated His promise on many occasions:

In Genesis 12:7a the Lord said to Abraham (then called Abram): "To your descendants I will give this land."

In Genesis 15:5c, the Lord had him look toward heaven and count the stars, saying to him, "So shall your descendants be."

In Genesis 17:4, the Lord said to him, "As for Me, behold, My covenant is with you, and you shall be a father of many nations."

Yet although Abraham first received God's promises at the age of seventy five, and although the Lord reaffirmed them to him many times, Abraham endured another *twenty-five years* of painful waiting before the promise came to pass. But on the day of his precious Isaac's birth, those years of waiting must have suddenly seemed as nothing, lost in the wonder and warmth of a newborn's love. Isaac might have been the first of a great nation, someone important to the very course of human history, but the precious child was also the tender object of a love kindled by twenty-five years of keen anticipation.

Could there ever have been a child more loved? Could there ever have been more doting parents? The lives of all new parents revolve around their infants, but how much more must that have been true of Abraham and Sarah, starting their second century of life as beginner parents?

Because of this, it is impossible to put into words the horror that Abraham must have felt when the Lord God issued this brief command:

> Now it came to pass after these things that God tested Abraham, and said to him, "Abraham!" And he said, "Here I am." Then He said, "Take now your son, your only son Isaac, whom you love, and go to the land of Moriah, and offer him there as a burnt offering on one of the mountains of which I shall tell you. (Gen. 22:1–2)

In thirty-seven brief words, the reality and extent of Abraham's surrender were put to the ultimate test as he was called upon to give his firstborn, the son more precious to him than life itself.

Yet in spite of the crushing weight that Abraham must have felt inside, his obedience was swift and complete. He did not hesitate for a moment, regardless of how he felt, for the Scripture declares, "So Abraham rose early in the morning and saddled his donkey, and took two of his young men with him, and Isaac his son; and he split the wood for the burnt offering, and arose and went to the place of which God had told him." (Gen. 22:3)

In fact, had God not stopped him, Abraham would have followed His command and sacrificed Isaac. The Scripture plainly states:

> Then they came to the place of which God had told him. And Abraham built an altar there and placed the

wood in order; and he bound Isaac his son and laid him on the altar, upon the wood. And Abraham stretched out his hand and took the knife to slay his son. But the Angel of the LORD called to him from heaven and said, "Abraham, Abraham!" So he said, "Here I am." And He said, "Do not lay your hand on the lad, or do anything to him. (Gen. 22:9–12a)

How could a father with as much love for his son as Abraham had for Isaac follow God's command to sacrifice him *without hesitation?* The answer is as simple as it is profound. Abraham had such great faith in the love of God that the Scripture declares, "By faith Abraham, when he was tested, offered up Isaac, and he who had received the promises offered up his only begotten son, of whom it was said, 'In Isaac your seed shall be called,' *concluding that God was able to raise him up, even from the dead,* from which he also received him in a figurative sense." (Heb. 11:18–19, emphasis added)

In other words, Abraham was so convinced of the goodness and power of God that he gave Him his complete trust, relying on God to make a way where there seemed to be none at all. You see, Abraham was "stuck" between the words of God. On the one hand, God had promised that Abraham would be the father of a great nation through a child borne by Sarah. Yet on the other hand, God had just as plainly spoken, enjoining him to sacrifice his child.

There was a time when instead of surrendering to the will of God, Abraham would have tried to take things into his hands and help God out. He learned the hard way that anything other than surrender brings hardship. You see, although Abraham had the promise of God that he would be the father of a great nation through Sarah, after years of waiting, they became impatient. So instead of *trusting* they began *trying,* deciding to give God a hand by devising their own solution.

Sarah gave her maidservant Hagar to Abraham, and soon the child Ishmael was produced by the union. Far from helping God, with the birth of Ishmael came a rival to the Father's plan, which was encapsulated in the birth of Isaac.

But Abraham learned his lesson. He learned to surrender—to let God be God. Abraham didn't try to reconcile the words that God had given him or make a way of his own devising. No, this time he would surrender and rely on God to make a way—and so He did.

Our God gave Abraham the best, but He also expected the best from Abraham without hesitation. This passage teaches us so much about tithing. You see, the Father's demand that Abraham sacrifice Isaac was in essence a demand that Abraham give Isaac to the Father as a tithe, for Isaac represented the *first* and the *best*.

Isaac was the first of a great nation; he was the apple of Abraham's eye and the focal point of all of his hopes. If one thing could vie with the Lord for first place in Abraham's heart, it was Isaac. And God had to know—more than that, Abraham and Isaac had to know—that God was first and there was no other. So the Lord demanded that Abraham give Isaac totally to Him.

I believe that God instituted tithing to raise *children*—not money—by giving His children an opportunity to demonstrate obedience, the kind of obedience that gives what is *best* and the kind of obedience that gives what is *first*. And when Abraham showed his willingness to give his first and his best, the Lord uttered these remarkable words, "Now I know that you fear God, since you have not withheld your son, your only son, from Me." (Gen. 22:12b)

What a strange thing for God to say when He had given Isaac to Abraham in the first place. Why would God say, "Now I know?" After all, He knew Abraham's heart inside out. And why would He test him if He did know? Why? Because your actions speak to heaven. Your actions declare to the angels and the invisible world your commitment to God. Like Abraham, your deeds of obedience allow the Father to say, "Now I know. Now I know you'll obey Me." God knows your heart, but your actions declare it loudly, not only to God but to the host of the invisible world watching you.

And when we take God at His word by obeying Him in love, He rewards us with abundance. We don't obey in order to receive His blessings; we obey because we love Him so much. Yet we know that our wonderful heavenly Father *will* bless us greatly, for it is in His nature. When we give our all, the Father gives it back to us and then some! That was certainly what the Father did with Abraham:

> Then Abraham lifted his eyes and looked, and there behind him was a ram caught in a thicket by its horns. So Abraham went and took the ram, and offered it up for a burnt offering instead of his son. And Abraham called the name of the place, The-Lord-Will-Provide; as it is said to this day, "In the Mount of the Lord it shall be provided." Then the Angel of the Lord called to Abraham a second time out of heaven, and said: "By Myself I have sworn, says the Lord, because you have done this thing, and have not withheld your son, your only son—blessing I will bless you, and multiplying I will multiply your descendants as the stars of the heaven and as the sand which is on the seashore; and your descendants shall possess the gate of their enemies. In your seed all the nations of the earth shall be blessed, because you have obeyed My voice." (Gen. 22:13–18)

Surrender: The Heart of the Matter

Nothing gets to the heart of the matter like the call to surrender. And there is no area where it is harder to fake surrender than in the area of our finances. I think Ron Blue was, so to speak, *right on the money* when he explained:

> [An] implication of believing that God owns it all is that stewardship cannot be faked. Prayer, Bible study, witnessing, fellowship, can all be faked—and anyone who has been a Christian for a relatively short period of time can fake any of them. But stewardship is revealed in one's checkbook. The checkbook reveals the use of God's resources in black and white. I often ask people to take out their checkbook, as it reveals much about the owner of the checkbook."[1]

I think this explains the remarkable encounter of Lord Jesus with the rich young ruler which is found in Mark 10:17–22:

> Now as He was going out on the road, one came running, knelt before Him, and asked Him, "Good Teacher, what shall I do that I may inherit eternal life?" So Jesus said to him, "Why do you call Me good? No one is good but One, that is, God. You know the commandments: 'Do not commit adultery,' 'Do not murder,' 'Do not steal,' 'Do not bear false witness,' 'Do not defraud,' 'Honor your father and your mother.' " And he answered and said to Him, "Teacher, all these things I have kept from my youth." Then Jesus, looking at him, loved him, and said to him, "One thing you lack: Go your way, sell whatever you have and give to the poor, and you will have treasure in heaven; and come, take up the cross, and follow Me." But he was sad at this word, and went away sorrowful, for he had great possessions.

Notice that the young man had a depth of spiritual insight. He recognized that Jesus was a good teacher. The Master Himself seized on the significance of the young man's words when He noted that only God is good. In other words, the young man recognized who Jesus was. We see confirmation of that in his actions toward the Lord—he *ran* up to Jesus and *fell at His knees*. The young man knew that he needed eternal life and that eternal life was found through Jesus, which is why he asked Jesus about how to inherit eternal life.

Notice also that the young man had a depth of obedience in his spiritual walk. When Jesus stated the commandments necessary to keep in order to merit eternal life, the young man said that lifestyle had been his practice since childhood. *And Jesus did not contradict him.*

Instead, Jesus looked at the young man who was zealous for eternal life and instantly, intuitively, "loved him." The Master loved the young man enough to help him understand what he was really like inside. It is so hard for us to actually gauge ourselves, which is why David cried out, "Who can discern his errors? Forgive my hidden faults." (Ps. 19:12 NIV) And so in great love, the Savior issued a challenge that cut through belief and action right down to the heart, "One thing you lack: Go your way, sell whatever you have and give to the poor, and you will have treasure in heaven; and come, take up the cross, and follow Me."

In that moment, and through the challenge to surrender in the area of finances, the Master helped the young man see the covetousness of his heart and his need for a Savior. This is one reason why obedience in the area of finances is so important, and why surrender manifests itself in the area of finances by giving our first and our best. When we give God our best, we show Him that we have surrendered to Him. When I give Him the first and best, I'm actually saying, "Everything else is Yours too."

Giving is really an expression of our commitment to

God. Giving is the deed and continual act that expresses our commitment to the Lord. We're saying, "What is mine is now Yours." When we give God the firstfruits, it's a declaration of our surrender to Him.

Surrender: Little Is Much When God Is in It

The miracle of the feeding of the five thousand often comes to mind when considering the mighty manifestations of the Lord Jesus. Jesus and the apostles had sought a remote place where they could rest. But the need that the multitudes felt for the Savior was such that they followed Him wherever He went. When they found Jesus, the Master responded to their need by teaching them about many things. Out in their remote location, the time passed quickly as the crowd sat and listened intently to the teachings of Jesus. Jesus had compassion on them and continued to teach them because their spiritual need was so acute. Before long, darkness was approaching.

Noting the lateness of the day, the disciples came to Jesus and suggested that He send the people away to the neighboring villages to buy bread, for many of them had eaten nothing all day long.

Jesus responded by saying, "You give them something to eat." But the cost to buy food far exceeded the resources available to the apostles. Furthermore, a quick check of this great throng of people, which was comprised of five thousand men as well as untold thousands of women and children, revealed that the total available food supply consisted of five small barley loaves and two small fish—the lunch of a single young boy.

What to do? Despair? Or surrender?

As the young boy surrendered all that he had to God, and as the apostles surrendered all of their doubts and rationalizations and obeyed the Savior's words, a great miracle began to unfold:

Then He commanded them to make them all sit down in groups on the green grass. So they sat down in ranks, in hundreds and in fifties. And when He had taken the five loaves and the two fish, He looked up to heaven, blessed and broke the loaves, and gave them to His disciples to set before them; and the two fish He divided among them all. So they all ate and were filled. And they took up twelve baskets full of fragments and of the fish. Now those who had eaten the loaves were about five thousand men. (Mark 6:39–44)

Imagine a crowd of five thousand men, plus women and children, being fed with only five loaves of bread and two fish. And then twelve baskets were left over after all of them had eaten their fill. What a miracle! When we surrender what we have to the Master, when we surrender our doubts and disbeliefs to the Lord, then and only then will we see the miraculous in our lives.

Surrender: The Secret

It is easy for us to think sometimes that we would surrender, especially in the area of finances, if our circumstances were different. "Once I get this bill paid," "Once I get a job," or "Once my children get out of school" are among the things we say to ourselves and to the Lord when it comes to surrender.

Yet the Scripture records a group of remarkable people who got beyond these excuses and so experienced joy unspeakable and full of glory. In 2 Corinthians 8–9, the apostle Paul talked about the generosity of the churches of Macedonia. But what is most remarkable is not the *fact* of their generosity as much as the *conditions* in which they were generous. One of the most amazing passages in all of Scripture is 2 Corinthians 8:2–3, which declares, "that in a great trial of affliction the abundance of their joy and their deep poverty abounded in the riches of their liberality. For I bear witness that according to their ability, yes, and beyond their ability, they were freely willing."

The very existence of the churches of Macedonia is a standing reproach to the "blab it and grab it" gospel. The words in the Greek translated "deep poverty" indicate that the Macedonians did not have enough to *survive*. Yet still they were able to experience such an amazing "abundance of joy" that they were able to collect a substantial offering for the church at Jerusalem. Think of it, that would be like taking an offering today among starving people in Ethiopia who not only gave far more than it appeared that they were able, but who actually begged to be able to participate in the privilege of giving.

The "Macedonian secret" to surrender was twofold: "they first gave themselves to the Lord" (8:5a). The Macedonians surrendered themselves completely to the Lord, but more than that, they surrendered themselves *to their spiritual leaders*, for the Scriptures declare, "They first gave themselves to the Lord, *and then to us by the will of God.*" (2 Cor 8:5, emphasis added)

The amazing joy experienced by the churches of Macedonia came from surrender to the Lord and to godly leadership. There was no question about cultic leadership, for the surrender of the Macedonians to their leaders was "by the will of God."

All too often in our congregations today men and women withhold their tithes because they take issue with the leadership. There is nothing spiritual in such a practice—far from it. If you cannot agree with your leaders and submit to their decisions, then find someplace where you can.

So you see, surrender is not about the circumstances *around us*. It's about the circumstances *within us*. When we surrender to the Lord and our God-ordained leadership, we can begin to experience Macedonian joy.

Surrender: The Right Perspective

Having the proper perspective of who we are as God's children, and the reason for God's blessings upon our lives, is vital. When we remember that we are to be stewards of what God has given—to serve as channels of blessing to others—it is so easy to give to the work of the Lord. For then what we give is not really ours in the first place but is just something the Lord has loaned to us.

When you have the right perspective, God will do wonderful and surprising things.

My crusade director told me of an incident that illustrates this principle so well. When he first began attending our church in the mid-1980s, he did not know the Lord. But as he heard the Word of God, he responded and invited Jesus Christ into his heart and life. He gave up his past and set his heart toward God.

Not long after his conversion, one Sunday morning his attention was directed to a gentleman sitting across the sanctuary. Right there in church God began to deal with him about giving the man his Rolex watch, the only thing of exceptional value that he still owned from his past life.

Not my watch, Lord! he thought, but the prompting would not go away. Finally, he struck a bargain with God: "If You move that man from way over there in the sanctuary, and bring him right here beside me, then I'll do it."

The praise and worship portion of the service continued. My crusade director forgot about the gentleman across the sanctuary and tried to concentrate on the words of the songs. When the music finally stopped and he turned to sit down, he was shocked to see the gentleman whom God had pointed out seated right next to him! Somehow, the man had moved from across the sanctuary to sit right next to him!

"Give him your Rolex," the Lord said again.

"All right, Lord, I give up. I'll obey."

Following the service, he told the man what had happened, explaining how the Lord had spoken to him and how he had struggled. Then he took off the Rolex watch and handed it to the gentleman. "The Lord told me to bless you with this, sir."

The man's eyes filled with tears as he began to share how the Lord had spoken to him before coming to church that day. He said that the Lord had promised him that someone was going to give him something in the service that would change his financial picture. The Rolex watch he now held was the fulfillment of that promise.

That's how God can use surrendered people.

Are you ready to experience the blessings of heaven to such a degree that you can't even contain them? Our heavenly Father's blessings are limitless and without measure. He is waiting to give them to His children. But first, in the holiness of this moment, you must surrender.

True Biblical Prosperity

After a terrible childhood illness robbed Helen Keller of sight and hearing, she embarked on a voyage of discovery to apprehend and then appreciate a world that was closed off to her by normal channels. It was the quest of a lifetime. She was able to discover without the aid of hearing or sight what is so easy to lose track of for those of us who can see and hear, and that is, "The best and most beautiful things in the world cannot be seen or even touched. They must be felt with the heart." What wisdom! You see, the prosperity God intends for you to enjoy isn't something you have in your *hand*; it's something you have in your *heart*.

In this chapter I want to show you the true nature of biblical prosperity. I'm afraid that *prosperity* is one of those words that has been hijacked by racketeers to such a degree that it has lost its dignity. But make no mistake about it, *the Bible does teach prosperity*, and I will not avoid teaching about it simply because the term and its truth are twisted. Winston Churchill once observed, "The great thing is to get the true picture, whatever it is." We're going to get the true picture of prosperity according to the Word of God. And with this understanding, I'm confident that you will begin to experience it in all of its fullness, which is just as the Father intends.

Biblical Prosperity

My friend, Biblical prosperity is about so much more than money. True Bible-based prosperity isn't centered on money. In its fullest meaning it really means "no lack," as the Scripture promises. No lack means having *all* your needs met in every area of your life.

Throughout the Bible, we find that men and women of God who lived in surrender to God experienced no lack. "No lack" is far different from "*no problems.*" Heroes of faith throughout the ages have experienced tremendous hardships, as the writer of the book of Hebrews so powerfully pointed out:

> Others were tortured, not accepting deliverance, that they might obtain a better resurrection. Still others had trial of mockings and scourgings, yes, and of chains and imprisonment. They were stoned, they were sawn in two, were tempted, were slain with the sword. They wandered about in sheepskins and goatskins, being destitute, afflicted, tormented—of whom the world was not worthy. They wandered in deserts and mountains, in dens and caves of the earth. (Heb. 11:35–38)

Yes, even in the midst of such terrible suffering, the provision of grace from the Lord meant that those heroes could experience no lack. Anyone can feel prosperous at the country club, but the miracle comes when you know His prosperity in the midst of persecution and deprivation.

Prophets and Prosperity

The heroes of faith of the old covenant experienced "no lack" without exception. While some were regarded as wealthy, others certainly were not. Yet they all lived a life of supernatural blessing, and so experienced no lack.

Abraham, David, and Solomon were men of wealth, social stature, and influence. Yet others were plainly not wealthy. Elijah, Elisha, and John the Baptist might not have been wealthy; nevertheless, they experienced abundance and had no lack because their needs were met supernaturally. For instance, after Elijah declared the word of the Lord to wicked King Ahab, God sent him to hide beside the brook Cherith. He drank fresh water from the brook, and the ravens fed him every morning and every evening. His needs were supernaturally met day after day. You could say it was "room service," for the Lord surely took care of him. Elijah experienced biblical prosperity.

Prosperity Through God's People

In the book of Acts, we see that the New Testament church had no lack, especially after Pentecost. Luke said of the church, "Nor was there anyone among them who lacked." (Acts 4:34) They were blessed and their needs were met.

But notice the mechanism God used to insure that they had no lack. Luke continued, "For all who were possessors of lands or houses sold them, and brought the proceeds of the things that were sold, and laid them at the apostles' feet; and they distributed to each as anyone had need." (Acts 4:34, 35) From time to time people in the church *did* have needs, but because of the faithfulness of God's people, the saints in need immediately had their needs met and so experienced no lack.

It is true that God delights to bless His people in unexpected ways. God's people *do* get unexpected checks in the mail. God's people *do* sometimes receive costly presents from strangers or people they barely know. These things happen, and you shouldn't be surprised when God blesses you in this way. But God has also ordained the Church, and when we are obedient in the area of giving, the Church can be the channel through which the Lord works to meet the needs of His children and thus insure that we have no lack.

That is why the apostle Paul was so zealous to collect the

offering for the church at Jerusalem. He explained in 2 Corinthians 8:13–15, where he declared:

> For I do not mean that others should be eased and you burdened; but by an equality, that now at this time your abundance may supply their lack, that their abundance also may supply your lack—that there may be equality. As it is written, "He who gathered much had nothing left over, and he who gathered little had no lack."

Prosperity: Through You and to You

Dr. E. V. Hill, a great preacher, dynamic man of God, and dear friend, once made a powerful statement that I have never forgotten: "If God can get it *through* you, God can get it *to* you. There is such balance in his statement.

You see, on the one hand, the Lord doesn't bless us so we can consume what we receive on our own lusts. On the other hand, the Lord doesn't expect us to be mere pipelines for blessings to flow through us to others without experiencing the blessing ourselves. When we are obedient to the Father, we use all that He gives us to bless others. And then because we are obedient children, the Father delights to bless *us*.

You don't have to worry about if or when the blessing is coming. In fact, He'll bless you so much that you'll say, "Lord, I can't handle it any more." You see, God wants to bless you far more than you want to be blessed. But the blessings of God do not come without cost. Before the blessings of the Father begin to be poured out upon your life, you must put yourself in the place where you can receive them. And that place is the place of *surrender*.

Prosperity Is More Than Wealth

Prosperity is the abundant, abiding presence of the Lord Jesus in a life. Jesus makes all the difference, and as Kathryn Kuhlman so wisely observed, "The poorest man with Jesus is rich, and the richest man without Him is poor." Knowing Him—and having a personal relationship with Jesus Christ—is the greatest blessing a person can know. Oh, how I love the truth expressed by Bill Gaither:

> *The longer I serve Him, the sweeter He grows.*
> *The more that I love Him, more love He bestows.*
> *Each day is like heaven, my heart overflows!*
> *The longer I serve Him, the sweeter He grows.*[1]

This is the abundance that our heavenly Father holds before each of us today and why it is so unfortunate when people spend so much time looking for material blessing that they overlook all the other manifestations of God's blessing happening around them. Worse than that, when people obsess on riches and seek only material wealth, they limit God because of their mistaken notion of what will bring happiness to their lives. True happiness comes only through surrender to the Father's will. When I surrender to Him, I will be blessed; He has promised to take care of me, and I know He will!

I want to devote the rest of this chapter to showing you just some of what constitutes true biblical prosperity, and the kinds of people the Lord prospers.

Prosperity Is Godliness with Contentment

The apostle Paul demonstrated this so clearly when he explained to young Timothy in 1 Timothy 6:6–10 where he declared:

> Now godliness with contentment is great gain. For we brought nothing into this world, and it is certain we can

carry nothing out. And having food and clothing, with these we shall be content. But those who desire to be rich fall into temptation and a snare, and into many foolish and harmful lusts which drown men in destruction and perdition. For the love of money is a root of all kinds of evil, for which some have strayed from the faith in their greediness, and pierced themselves through with many sorrows.

When you possess godliness *and* contentment, you are truly prosperous, for you are living a life destined to bring a reward *and* you are happy on the journey. By contrast, the apostle Paul noted that the way of seeking prosperity through riches is one that only "drowns men in destruction and perdition, piercing them through with many griefs."

With contentment, you enjoy a prosperity that is independent of your circumstances. It is the kind of contentment the apostle Paul testified to when he declared, "I have learned in whatever state I am, to be content: I know how to be abased, and I know how to abound. Everywhere and in all things I have learned both to be full and to be hungry, both to abound and to suffer need. I can do all things through Christ who strengthens me." (Phil. 4:11–13) With this mighty power of Christ, prosperity becomes something within you, not something you have to grasp and maintain. When you enjoy this prosperity, you become fearless in your prayer life, as Phillips Brooks exhorted:

> O, do not pray for easy lives; pray to be stronger men!
> Do not pray for tasks equal to your powers; pray for powers equal to your tasks.
> Then the doing of your work shall be no miracle, but you shall be the miracle.

Plato said, "The greatest wealth is to live content with little." But the Scriptures go one better: the greatest wealth is to be content with prosperity—*true biblical prosperity,* that is. This prosperity comes not from hog futures, but from delighting yourself in the Lord, and so allowing Him to give you the desires of your heart.

Prosperity Is Enjoyment

Most people have to take for granted what others say about enjoying life. For instance, it is easy to think that we would really enjoy life if we were millionaires. Of course, most of us will never be millionaires, so we have to take somebody else's word about whether being a millionaire results in enjoying life.

King Solomon, on the other hand, was able to fully pursue and experience everything that is said to bring enjoyment in life. He knew the outcome of riches, intelligence, hard work, military conquest, and sensual indulgence—and wrote about all of these things very candidly in the book of Ecclesiastes.

Having experienced all of these things, his insight in Ecclesiastes 3:12–13 (NIV, emphasis added) is remarkable:

" *I know that there is nothing better for men than to be happy and do good* while they live. That everyone may eat and drink, and find satisfaction in all his toil— *this is the gift of God.*" This is Solomon's central theme, and he returns to it again and again because it is so important: " *So I commend the enjoyment of life,* because nothing is better for a man under the sun than to eat and drink and be glad. Then joy will accompany him in his work all the days of the life God has given him under the sun." (Eccl. 8:15 NIV, emphasis added)

There is nothing greater than to enjoy life. But enjoyment doesn't automatically or even often come from riches, accomplishment, intelligence, hard work, or sensual indulgence. No enjoyment comes from God, and with this gift we find satisfaction in what we do and what we have. And finding this enjoyment, we are truly and thoroughly prosperous regardless of our circumstances.

Prosperity Is No Lack

When the Scriptures talk about "no lack," when they hold before us the prospect of having all of our needs met, it is important to realize that this only (and barely) begins to describe the kind of blessing the Father bestows upon His obedient children. Remember, there is no scarcity with God. He doesn't need to ration blessings so that He will have enough to go around.

No, when we enjoy biblical abundance, we experience the truth the apostle Paul spoke of in 2 Corinthians 9:8–11 (NIV), where he promised:

> And God is able to make all grace abound to you, so that in all things at all times, having all that you need, you will abound in every good work. As it is written:
> "He has scattered abroad his gifts to the poor;
> his righteousness endures forever."
> Now he who supplies seed to the sower and bread for food will also supply and increase your store of seed and will enlarge the harvest of your righteousness. You will be made rich in every way so that you can be generous on every occasion, and through us your generosity will result in thanksgiving to God."

Prosperity Is the Fruit of the Spirit

When the blessed Holy Spirit is resident and active in our lives, we know the abundance of the fruit of the Spirit, which the apostle Paul listed for us in Galatians 5:22–23 (NIV): "The fruit of the Spirit is love, joy, peace, patience, kindness, goodness, faithfulness, gentleness and self-control." Although the apostle Paul concluded with, "*Against such there is no law*," let me add, *And on these things no price can be placed. The fruit of the Spirit cannot be purchased, yet the Lord prospers us with them when we surrender to Him.*

Wealth Is Less Than Prosperity

I haven't even touched on many other elements of prosperity, such as,

- Salvation (John 3:16)
- An eternal inheritance (Ps. 37:18)
- Protection (2 Chron. 16:9)
- Answers to prayer (Ps. 20:6)
- Reward (1 Cor. 3)
- Preservation (Ps. 145:20)
- Victory (1 Cor. 15:57)
- Strength (Ps. 18:2)
- Deliverance (Ps. 18:17)
- Health (Ps. 103:3)

Not one of these can be purchased, yet all of them are part of true biblical prosperity and come from the gracious hand of our wonderful, prospering Lord!

Who Prospers?

To grasp the full dimensions of true biblical prosperity, we have to understand not only what prosperity is, but also the kinds of people God blesses with prosperity. The Sermon on the Mount (Matt. 5–7), the Savior's inaugural address, begins with what are commonly referred to as the Beatitudes. In only a few verses, the Master drew a passionate portrait of those who will experience true biblical prosperity and what that prosperity entails.

Prosperous People Are Poor in Spirit

Blessed are the poor in spirit,
For theirs is the kingdom of heaven. (Matt. 5:3)

When Jesus said the "poor in spirit" are blessed, He was referring to people who depend upon the Lord for every need in life. The poor in spirit freely acknowledge their dependence on their heavenly Father and rely on Him for their daily sustenance and for every need.

When the Holy Spirit revealed to me what being "poor in spirit" really meant, it affected my life deeply. Only as we come to the end of ourselves and depend on the Lord do we become poor in spirit. For some reason, something inside us wants to do just about everything independently of God. Yet all too often we fall flat on our faces when we attempt to function in our own strength and abilities. Then we come to the realization that we can do nothing on our own. Then we confess with the prophet Zechariah:

"Not by might nor by power, but by My Spirit,"
Says the LORD of hosts. (Zech. 4:6b)

David du Plessis, who was called "Mr. Pentecost," was a great inspiration to me in the early days of my ministry. I had been preaching for about one year, and I was attending a conference in Brockville, Ontario, Canada, where he was speaking. He and I were walking down a hallway one evening after he had preached a powerful message on forgiveness. I was really looking forward to getting him alone and learning the secrets of ministry from his years of experience.

As we walked along, I said, "Dr. du Plessis, I want to ask you a question: How can I please God?" I shall *never* forget his reply. The dear man took his finger, stuck it in my chest, and pushed me up against the wall, all the while saying in a serious tone, "Young man, it's not *your* ability; it's *His* ability in *you*. Good night!" And with that he left me in the hallway and proceeded to his room. I have to tell you that I was shell-shocked, but oh, what he taught me about being poor in spirit!

It is not our ability. It is not our strength. It is absolutely not us. There's not a single thing we can do to win God's grace or merit His favor—absolutely nothing. His grace is freely offered, and we only have to accept it. Chances are, you already understand this, but when you truly grasp this truth in the very depth of your being, that "in me (that is, in my flesh) nothing good dwells" (Rom. 7:18a), and that you have nothing to offer Him, you know the prosperity that comes from being poor in spirit. Then the kingdom of heaven is truly yours.

Prosperous People Are Those Who Mourn

> Blessed are those who mourn,
> For they shall be comforted." (Matt. 5:4)

King David was a man after God's own heart. And like anyone who has a personal encounter with our holy God, David was keenly aware not only of his own righteousness but of his utter unworthiness in light of the blazing purity and perfection of the Almighty. When we really encounter the Master, our passion becomes not to advance ourselves and guard our reputation, but rather to find cleansing and forgiveness for our ever-obvious sin.

We see this in David's heart cry in Psalm 40:11–13 (emphasis added), where he cries out:

> Do not withhold Your tender mercies from me, O
> LORD;
> Let Your lovingkindness and Your truth continually
> preserve me.
> For innumerable evils have surrounded me;
> *My iniquities have overtaken me,* so that I am not able to
> look up;
> They are more than the hairs of my head;
> Therefore my heart fails me.
> Be pleased, *O LORD, to deliver me;*
> *O LORD, make haste to help me!*

He was crying out (mourning) for deliverance from his own sins.

And such cries move the heart of the Father. While the trappings of the Pharisees impressed people around them, it was the unaffected cry, "God, be merciful to me, a sinner," of a man so broken by his sin that he wouldn't even look toward heaven that moved the Father's heart and does so today. (Luke 18:9–14)

That was what Jesus meant when He said, "Blessed are those who mourn." He wasn't talking about an emotional mourning or a physical mourning. He was talking about a spiritual mourning, brokenness before the Lord.

David declared, "A broken and a contrite heart . . . thou wilt not despise." (Ps. 51:17 KJV) David was repentant and brokenhearted over his sin. When we mourn, we yearn, long for, and desire in our hearts that our whole lives conform to the image of Jesus. As you and I confront the traits and tendencies in our lives that are unlike those in His life, the Holy Spirit *prospers* us by bringing comfort in our brokenness, for there we allow Him to reshape the personality into the likeness of our Lord and Savior.

And this is prosperity! When we sin, when we hurt others and ourselves, when we bring shame on the God who loves us, no amount of money can change the fact or turn back the clock. And it doesn't matter how much we "forgive ourselves" or other people tell us that what we've done is acceptable or justifiable. What we need—and what only God can provide—is the assurance of forgiveness, once we ask Him for that forgiveness and come with a broken spirit. This was why David extolled with joy:

> Blessed is he whose transgression is forgiven,
> Whose sin is covered.
> Blessed is the man to whom the LORD does not impute iniquity,
> And in whose spirit there is no deceit.

When I kept silent, my bones grew old
Through my groaning all the day long.
For day and night Your hand was heavy upon me;
My vitality was turned into the drought of summer.

Selah

I acknowledged my sin to You,
And my iniquity I have not hidden.
I said, "I will confess my transgressions to the LORD,"
And You forgave the iniquity of my sin.   Selah
For this cause everyone who is godly shall pray to You
In a time when You may be found;
Surely in a flood of great waters
They shall not come near him.
You are my hiding place;
You shall preserve me from trouble;
You shall surround me with songs of deliverance.

Selah. (Ps. 32:1–7)

Prosperous People Are the Meek

Blessed are the meek,
For they shall inherit the earth. (Matt. 5:5)

For some reason it is so hard for us to comprehend the biblical concept of meekness. Because of this, I suspect that many confuse meekness with timidity. Meekness is *not* weakness. Meekness doesn't mean being housebroken like some pet. No, it refers to the quality of living that is free of pride, aggressiveness, or self-assertiveness. It is an attitude that comes from the settled decision to submit your life to God, think His thoughts, and make His will your will. Meekness as Jesus taught is the expression of your deepest desire and strongest faith to obey God.

When you are meek, you are secure in the calling the Lord has given you. You have no need to jockey for position, promote your own interests, or defend yourself. No, you know that you are secure in the will of God, and that He will protect, promote, and prosper you.

I know of no better illustration of this in the Scripture than Numbers 12. Moses had the call of God on his life. He knew who he was in the Lord, and with the knowledge came humility, or meekness. (v. 3) By contrast, Moses' relatives, Miriam and Aaron, felt that they were undervalued and underutilized. But instead of taking their concerns to the Lord, they promoted themselves, saying, "Has the LORD indeed spoken only through Moses? Has He not spoken through us also?" (v. 2)

Moses' own brother and sister were basically saying, "Well, who do you think you are? God can use us as well as He can use you." Now the thing that makes this passage such a remarkable illustration of meekness *and the prosperity that comes from meekness* is what comes next. The passage says, "And the LORD heard it." Moses didn't need to point out to God what was happening. No, the Lord was on watch for Moses, protecting him. Moses didn't even need to get *angry* about the situation. No, the Lord did that for him as well. In fact, verse 9 declares that the anger of the Lord *burned* against them, and the Lord judged them and struck Miriam with leprosy. (v. 10)

And because the Lord protected Moses, as a meek man he was free to plead to the Lord to be merciful to Miriam and Aaron. If there's a better illustration of strength under control, I don't know what it is. The easiest thing in the world would have been for Moses to have said, "*All right!* You messed with me, and now God has judged you. Sit back and enjoy it!" But instead, Moses showed the power of meekness when he called out to the Lord, "Please heal her, O God, I pray!" (v. 13)

Moses was *meek* and you could say that in this situation he *inherited*. He kept his position and was decisively vindicated by the Lord. Miriam and Aaron were assertive and did not achieve what they wanted. Make no mistake, the meek enjoy the prosperity that will culminate with *inheriting the earth.*

Prosperous People Hunger and Thirst After Righteousness

> Blessed are those who hunger and thirst for
> righteousness,
> For they shall be filled. (Matt. 5:6)

All of us are driven by our desires—voices that call out to us, sometimes with great urgency, other times with great subtlety. Sometimes they force us in a certain direction like the sharp point of a spear in the small of the back. Other times they gently but persistently nudge us in a direction like an insistent breeze against an automobile. There are many different kinds of desires and many different intensities. But all kinds of desires share one thing in common: they cannot be satisfied. Once desire achieves its object, it switches to the next object. As it relates to the desire for fame, Lily Tomlin expressed it in a humorous way, "I always wanted to be somebody. Now I see I should have been more specific."

Desire always wants something more. For instance:

A child dreams one day of playing little league baseball.
He plays Little League and dreams one day of playing baseball in college.
He plays baseball in college and dreams one day of playing professional baseball.
He plays professional baseball and dreams one day of playing in the all-star game.
He plays in the all-star game and dreams one day of being inducted into the Hall of Fame.
He is inducted into the Hall of Fame and dreams of being regarded the best player of all time.

He is regarded as the best player of all time and dreams
. . .

As the expression goes:

Been there.
Done that.
Now what?

This is what so many people fail to understand about
prosperity. They think they will be happy with one more
thing, one more relationship, or one more accomplishment. They're discontent because they do not have it. They
spend (miserable) years getting it. Then when they get it,
they find that it wasn't all that it was cracked up to be. So
desire focuses on something else.

This is why the Bible emphasizes *contentment* as opposed
to aggrandizement. Truly prosperous people set their desire
on *righteousness*, for they know that it is our sure inheritance
through faith in the Lord Jesus. The apostle Paul declares in
2 Corinthians 5:18–21, "that God was in Christ reconciling
the world to Himself, not imputing their trespasses to
them. . . . For He made Him who knew no sin to be sin for
us, that we might become the righteousness of God in
Him."

You see, prosperity isn't having more stuff, it's being
filled. And it is the promise of God for all who hunger and
thirst after His righteousness.

Prosperous People Are Merciful

Blessed are the merciful,
For they shall obtain mercy. (Matt. 5:7)

When we meet the Lord, we are overwhelmed by the
forgiveness He extends to us. The simple words of the apos-

tle Paul in 2 Corinthians 5:19 can't even begin to hint at the costliness and wonder of the gift of salvation we have through the sacrifice of the Lord Jesus, "that God was in Christ reconciling the world to Himself, not imputing their trespasses to them."

The moment you find the Lord, a *glorious* transformation occurs. As you encounter and experience His love and mercy, it is only natural that you begin to extend mercy to others. You become a forgiving person. You take on the nature of the Lord Himself, for now you become loving and kind yourself. The Bible says, "Freely ye have received, freely give." (Matt. 10:8 KJV) You actually become an extension of the Lord to others—an ambassador of reconciliation. (2 Cor. 5:20)

The merciful then experience the wonderful prosperity of receiving mercy. They not only receive this from the Savior who delights in their obedience, but also from those around them as they receive the mercy they have extended to others.

Prosperous People Are Pure in Heart

> Blessed are the pure in heart,
> For they shall see God. (Matt. 5:8)

The purity that Jesus referred to is so much more than a mere outward show of religiosity. For purity to exist, it must flow from our innermost being and command the very core of our personality. When we have a pure heart, living our lives in a way pleasing to the Father becomes our central concern.

Kathryn Kuhlman once shared that she often said in prayer, "Lord, if there is anything in me You don't want, just take it out and kill it." That's really what it is to be pure in heart: a passion to be pure before the Lord and live a holy life. We hunger for holiness when we say, "Lead me closer to you, Lord." This passion for purity is really a manifestation of gratitude to God. I believe R. T. Kendall is right when he observes, "Holy living is a way of saying, 'Thank You, Lord, for saving my soul.'"

Those who are pure in heart enjoy the special kind of prosperity that comes from seeing God. The apostle John declared in John 1:18, "No one has seen God at any time. The only begotten Son, who is in the bosom of the Father, He has declared Him." Thus, the pure in heart are blessed with a "face-to-face" intimacy with God through the Lord Jesus now, and the blessing of standing before Him in eternity.

Prosperous People Are Peacemakers

> Blessed are the peacemakers,
> For they shall be called [the children] of God.
> (Matt. 5:9)

Anyone who is engaged in bringing peace is in a noble profession. Yet the best way to bring peace is from the inside out. It happens as people find Jesus Christ as their Lord and Savior. The peacemakers who experience the biblical prosperity referred to here have as their chief goal the reconciliation of lost and suffering people to the Lord. Salvation brings peace between wayward children and their loving Father.

And for these special peace-bringers, God holds out the prosperity of being known as His children. There is a power in the lives of men and women who are about the business of leading people to faith in the Lord Jesus. They have a depth to their lives, a magnetism to their spirits, and a power to their words. The apostle Paul pointed toward this when he quoted the declaration of Isaiah, "How beautiful are the feet of those who preach the gospel of peace,/Who bring glad tidings of good things!" (Rom. 10:15)

Prosperous People Are Persecuted for Righteousness' Sake

> Blessed are those who are persecuted for
>   righteousness' sake,
> For theirs is the kingdom of heaven.
> Blessed are you when they revile and persecute you,
> and say all kinds of evil against you falsely for My
> sake. Rejoice and be exceedingly glad, for great is
> your reward in heaven, for so they persecuted the
> prophets who were before you." (Matt. 5:10–12)

The moment you surrender to the Lord, the moment you look at your sin through the eyes of the Savior, the moment you exchange your power for His, seek Him with all of your heart, and commit yourself to helping others know the Lord, *opposition will arise against you.*

Prosperity isn't a lukewarm, plain vanilla life. Prosperity is the blessing of God that means that *your life will count.* If your life is free from turbulence, then you're not in the place of blessing—you're on the sidelines. You're missing abundant life now and a rewarded life then. Prosperity doesn't mean an absence of trouble; it means a great future reward *for* your trouble.

It means that you have taken your place in that high and holy fellowship, the succession of God's servants stretching back to the prophets who were persecuted for righteousness' sake. It means that you are part of a chosen fraternity who will enjoy God's presence for eternity. This is the highest form of prosperity, and the one the apostle Paul strove for so mightily, as he declared in Philippians 3:7–15:

> But what things were gain to me, these I have counted
> loss for Christ. Yet indeed I also count all things loss for
> the excellence of the knowledge of Christ Jesus my
> Lord, for whom I have suffered the loss of all things,
> and count them as rubbish, that I may gain Christ and

be found in Him, not having my own righteousness, which is from the law, but that which is through faith in Christ, the righteousness which is from God by faith; that I may know Him and the power of His resurrection, *and the fellowship of His sufferings, being conformed to His death, if, by any means, I may attain to the resurrection from the dead.* Not that I have already attained, or am already perfected; but I press on, that I may lay hold of that for which Christ Jesus has also laid hold of me. Brethren, I do not count myself to have apprehended; but one thing I do, forgetting those things which are behind and reaching forward to those things which are ahead, I press toward the goal for the prize of the upward call of God in Christ Jesus. Therefore *let us, as many as are mature, have this mind*; and if in anything you think otherwise, God will reveal even this to you.

Prosperity and You

Oliver Wendell Holmes wisely observed, "I find that the great thing in this world is not so much where we stand, as in what direction we are moving." I know that like me, you want to move toward biblical prosperity; you want the fullness of the Father's blessing to be manifested in your life. The Lord showers this prosperity upon His obedient children, and an extremely important area of obedience is the whole area of giving. As you prayerfully study and obey the powerful principles found in these next few chapters, be prepared to experience biblical prosperity as *never* before.

CHAPTER 6

Giving as the Father Desires

A donation in the amount of $266 arrived at the ministry recently. Most monetary gifts we receive are in even, round figures. Consequently, a gift of $266 appeared unusual and caught the attention of one of my associate pastors.

During a follow-up telephone call, he discovered the story behind the $266 gift. It seems the couple had at one time experienced some financial setbacks and had incurred heavy debt. They explained that the $266 represented all the money they had, and because it wasn't enough to pay off any one of their bills or even make a dent in what they owed, they decided to give the money in its entirety to the Lord and trust Him for their needs.

Within just weeks of their giving the money, a most amazing miracle took place. Oil was discovered on their property, even though oil was not usually found in their area of the country. An oil company negotiated a contract with them for the rights to the oil. The contract assured them an income from the oil of $5,000 a month! And besides the unexpected blessing of $5,000 a month from the existing oil, they were about to start drilling for more oil in other locations on their property.

They said they had given everything they had, and God had blessed them beyond anything they had ever experienced. To truly please the Lord, we must give in the *manner* He calls for, and use the *method* He calls for.

The Manner God Calls For

Give Totally, Dying to Self

Dietrich Bonhoeffer, a German Christian slain by the Nazis, said, "When Jesus bids us come to Him, He bids us come and die." In Chapter 4, I talked about how important surrender is on the biblical road to blessing. Yet ultimately, surrender means that we must die to ourselves.

Think of it—a man who surrenders all and dies to himself owns absolutely nothing. He is dead! He says, "God, my life is Yours, my home is Yours, my children are Yours, everything I have is Yours. And since it's all Yours, I'm holding nothing back. I give it all willingly to You, Lord." And at that moment the ownership has changed, and a new Master is in charge.

The moment this death takes place, giving begins. People who cannot give haven't died yet. Here is a statement I want you to consider carefully: *only the dead give; the living don't.* If I fail to surrender totally to God and I continue to hold on to things, I am really saying, "Mine, mine, mine, mine," and I am not dead at all. But when lust and greed are dead, giving takes place.

Just what is this death I've been describing? How do I die that I might live? How do I surrender that I might be blessed? What is true death to self? Jesus gave us the answers to these questions.

In John 12, we read how some people came to Philip and asked, "Sir, we wish to see Jesus." (v. 21)

We can make no greater request than to say, "We wish to see Jesus." Here is what the Master said, "Unless a grain of wheat falls into the ground and dies, it remains alone; but if it dies, it produces much grain." (John 12:24)

What an answer! "Unless a grain of wheat falls into the ground and dies, it remains alone." If it doesn't die, it abides alone. But if it's willing to die and be sown, it will bring forth much fruit.

Each year on December 7, I reflect on what happened on that date in 1974. I can still remember that first night as I stood on the platform in the basement of a Pentecostal church in Oshawa, Ontario, Canada, and preached my first sermon. I had suffered with a stammering tongue for all of my twenty-one years, but in a split second God healed my stammering as I began to preach and proclaim His Word with liberty that I had never known before.

Today I look back and realize that I am still learning what Jesus said in John 12:24: If that seed doesn't die, it can't produce. If that seed doesn't die, it abides alone.

As long as I tried on my own—in my flesh—to speak clearly, I stammered. Sometimes I tried so hard to speak that I became totally tongue-tied and couldn't even be understood. In those moments I became so embarrassed that I just wanted to disappear! But when I finally gave up, surrendered my stuttering to the Lord, and died to myself, the miracle came. To God be all the glory!

One of the great truths of the kingdom of God is this: death *must* occur before renewed life is possible. In the natural a seed must give its life and plunge into the dark death of the soil before the increase can sprout, grow, and be harvested. And just as the increase is harvested in the natural, so the same principles apply in the area of giving.

This principle of death preceding true life is illustrated repeatedly in the lives of many Bible heroes.

Abraham and Death to Self

I've already written much in this book about the founding father of our faith, Abraham. What I haven't discussed is how Abram died—not his final physical demise, but his death to self. When God called Abram (Gen. 12) to come out of his country to a land He would show him, his death to self began. But it was just the beginning of the death process, for so much of Abram was still alive that God had to deal with him.

When Abram came to the promised land, rather than staying there, he went down to Egypt because he faced a famine and began to doubt. Later he questioned God by saying, "What will You give me, seeing I go childless?" (Gen. 15:2) God had already told him he would father a child, but Abram had not died to his unbelief. Then Sarah and Abram worked together on the Hagar fiasco—trying "to help God." It was clear that Abram was still very much alive. Remember, if you think you can help God, you're definitely not dead yet!

Finally, when Abram was almost a century old, something glorious happened. The Lord appeared to him and said, "I am Almighty God; walk before Me and be blameless. . . . No longer shall your name be called Abram, but your name shall be Abraham; for I have made you a father of many nations." (Gen. 17:1b, 5)

Abram was ninety nine years old. Why did God wait so long to fulfill His promise? Why wasn't Abram's name changed before that time? I believe it was because the Lord did not reveal Himself to Abram as God almighty until Abram's flesh was too weak for him to trust in anymore. Only when Abram realized that it was not by might, it was not by power, it was not by ability, it was not by intelligence, it was not by education, it was not by training, but it was " *by My Spirit, saith the Lord,*" was Abram ready for a new name and a new surrendered life.

And when Abram died to the flesh, God said, "You are no longer Abram. You are Abraham." The very nature and breath of God entered into his life. Then and only then did Isaac come.

Remember this vital principle: *the promise will not come as long as the flesh is alive.*

Abram became Abraham when he died to self. And that death to self finally came when Abram discovered that he could not produce physically. Some have asked, "How many years did Abram wait for God's promise to be fulfilled?" But that is really not the question. The real question is, How long did *God* wait?

God promised that Isaac would come, and He never wavered from that promise. But Isaac was not born by the strength of the flesh, for Abraham's flesh by that time was unable to father a child. Isaac was born by the strength of God's promise. But the promise of God could not be fulfilled as long as Abraham's flesh was alive.

Death to flesh is a most difficult thing. The flesh cannot be converted; the flesh cannot be saved. That's why the only safe place for you and me is the cross!

The cross is our place of safety. There our flesh is crucified so that true, Spirit-breathed life may come. Just as with Abraham, the moment we are dead, then God is free to bless us.

Joseph and Death to Self

Joseph was another hero of faith who first had to die to self and to the flesh. Though he was just a young man, God spoke to him through a dream and said, "One day you will rule on a throne and will be a great man." Not long after that, Joseph called his brothers together and reported that one day they were all going to bow down before him.

His father, Jacob, naturally got upset with him and said, "How dare you tell your brothers that we are all going to bow down to you?"

Joseph, lacking discretion, couldn't wait to tell his brothers about his dream. The dream would come to pass— but only after Joseph died to self. And my friend, death is *never* easy. Joseph had to experience the horrors of betrayal and enslavement, the outrage and shame of false accusation, and finally the wrenching despair of prison before he learned how to die to self.

The death process for Joseph began in earnest while he

was in prison. He had been dying to self all along, but still there was enough of his flesh gasping for life that God wasn't ready to use him. Even from his prison cell Joseph was looking for some recognition when he said to his fellow inmate, the butler, "Make sure you tell Pharaoh about me, please. Be certain to tell him that I exist." I think you'll agree that anyone seeking recognition and promotion isn't dead yet!

Because of that, God made sure that the butler did not mention Joseph to Pharaoh after his release from prison. So Joseph once again found himself forgotten, languishing in prison, day by day feeling life pass him by. Then one day, in the secret recesses of his heart, Joseph came to the end of himself, surrendered to God, and in dying to self found the life that God had ordained for him before the very beginning of time.

Pharaoh had a disturbing dream, a dream that he knew was more than a random jumble of thoughts at the end of a busy day. The dream had a meaning—a meaning he had to discover no matter what the cost. And as Pharaoh desperately sought for someone who could interpret the dream, it was then that God caused the butler to remember an interpreter of dreams from long ago. Joseph had died totally to self, and in so doing he became totally alive to the purposes of God.

When I used to listen to Kathryn Kuhlman speak, I often heard her say things like, "I died a long time ago," or "I die every time I walk onto a platform." Her statements perplexed me, and I wondered to myself, *What is she talking about? What does she mean that she died a long time ago?*

But I knew there was something significant to her words. And so in my own zealousness to experience all of God and be used by him I used to pray, "God, please kill me!" When I think about those days, I can only shake my head and laugh. But now by His grace, I understand what she was referring to—and it is such a precious truth!

I now know that the most anointed people on earth are dead. Not dead physically, but dead to the things of this world. And I've discovered that God anoints only "dead people" because in dying to self, we become fully alive to the will and way of the Master.

Moses and Death to Self

And consider Moses, whom God sent into the wilderness. He experienced isolation and exile, raising sheep for his father-in-law on the backside of the desert. There he learned to die to himself and his ambition.

When God presented Himself to Moses at Horeb, the one-time prince had lost his position, his influence, and in the natural the best years of his life. He might have been eighty years old, but he "was a very humble man, more humble than anyone else on the face of the earth." (Num. 12:3 NIV) In other words, Moses had died to self. In other words, *he was just the man God was looking for.*

And from the encounter with the burning bush to his glimpse at death of the fair vistas of the promised land, the greatest revelation ever experienced by any human being came to Moses after he died to self.

God isn't looking for "a few good men"—he's looking for a few *dead* men—men and women who understand from experience the might and mystery of the apostle Paul's majestic words in 2 Corinthians 5:14–17, where he declares:

> For the love of Christ compels us, because we judge thus: that if One died for all, then all died; and He died for all, that those who live should live no longer for themselves, but for Him who died for them and rose again. Therefore, from now on, we regard no one according to the flesh. Even though we have known Christ according to the flesh, yet now we know Him thus no longer. Therefore, if anyone is in Christ, he is a new

creation; old things have passed away; behold, all things have become new.

Give the First and Best

God not only *deserves* our first and best gift—throughout the pages of Scripture we can see that He *demands* it. Abraham was a very prosperous man with abundant livestock and a burgeoning household. Yet none of it meant anything to him in comparison to his dear son, his child of promise—precious Isaac. Yet it was precisely Isaac that God demanded, and it was Isaac that Abraham willingly offered.

Yahweh God chose Moses to deliver His people and reveal His laws. Throughout the more than six-hundred laws, voluminous and diverse as they are, yet still there is one message that runs through them from start to finish, "The Lord wants the first of everything. The first of your children, the first of your sons, the first of your sheep, the first of your goats, the first of your fortune—the first of *everything*."

King David, that sweet singer of Israel and a man after God's own heart, knew his heavenly Father well enough to resolve, "I will not give what has cost me nothing." (2 Sam. 24:24) No, for God only the first and the best would do.

When we give God our *best*, we show Him that we have surrendered to Him. When we give Him the *first* and *best*, we're actually saying, "You can take whatever You want. Everything else is Yours too." Giving is really an outward expression of our inner commitment to God. Giving God what is first and best is the plainest possible declaration that "what is mine is now Yours." Giving God our firstfruits is nothing less than a full declaration of our complete surrender to Him.

Give in Recognition of the Law of Sowing and Reaping

"For whatever a man sows, that he will also reap." (Gal. 6:7b) In nine simple words the Scripture describes what might be the most powerful and pervasive principle of life on earth. The law of sowing and reaping is as universal as gravity, as relentless as friction, and as inevitable as death and taxes. Every single moment of every single day as long as we live, the law of sowing and reaping is working either for us or against us—*in every area of life*—dependent on what we sow as ordained by God almighty.

And this is a good thing, for it gives us the encouragement that our heavenly Father *will* bless and reward our faithful work for Him. For in God's providence, we not only reap what we sow, we reap *more* than what we sow. We see this in the life of Isaac when the Scripture declares in Genesis 26:12, "Then Isaac sowed in that land, and reaped in the same year a hundredfold; and the Lord blessed him." How encouraging it is to know that in sowing love, we shall surely reap love; that in sowing mercy, we shall surely reap mercy; that in sowing kindness, we shall surely reap kindness!

Not that sowing is easy, far from it. And while it is important to sow with the harvest in view, it is also sometimes true that the harvest is a long time coming. But this only serves to make the harvest that much sweeter when it does come, for the Scriptures declare in Psalm 126:5–6, emphasis added:

Those who sow in tears
Shall reap in joy.
He who continually goes forth weeping,
Bearing seed for sowing,
Shall doubtless come again with rejoicing,
Bringing his sheaves with him.

This was the great encouragement that the apostle Paul held out to the Corinthians to convince them to make good on their pledges for the church in Jerusalem:

And God is able to make all grace abound toward you, that you, always having all sufficiency in all things, may have an abundance for every good work. . . . Now may He who supplies seed to the sower, and bread for food, supply and multiply the seed you have sown and increase the fruits of your righteousness, while you are enriched in everything for all liberality, which causes thanksgiving through us to God. (2 Cor. 9:8, 10–11)

Of course, we do have a choice. We can give sparingly, certain in the knowledge that what we receive out of life will be just as sparing, as the apostle Paul predicted in 2 Corinthians 9:6, "But this I say: He who sows sparingly will also reap sparingly, and he who sows bountifully will also reap bountifully." And I pray that your choice will *always* be to sow bountifully.

Now before I get too far into this teaching, like you, I recognize that the law of sowing and reaping has been twisted by some people to mean something far different from what I am talking about here.

God wants you to give to His work because you *love Him*, because you *want to please Him*. But *He* loves *you* so much that you know that as you give in love, He will shower His best upon you. This is giving as the Father intends; this is giving with the harvest in mind. You don't give to receive, but you give in *expectation* of receiving. That is where faith in God is involved. It's not a business deal. It's not gambling. It's believing God's promise. He declared, "Give, and it will be given to you." (Luke 6:38)

Few preachers are as well known for their teaching on sowing and reaping as my dear friend, Dr. Oral Roberts. One of the most amazing lessons I learned about the principles of sowing and reaping came through him following a service at the church I pastor in Orlando, Florida.

"Benny," Dr. Roberts said to me, "can I talk to you like a son?"

"Certainly, Dr. Roberts," I answered.

"*You take lousy offerings*!" he said firmly.

I'm sure that my face betrayed how surprised I was by his comment. He and I had just retired to my study after concluding a wonderful service in which he had delivered a dynamic, anointed message.

"What do you mean, Dr. Roberts?" I asked slowly.

"*You take lousy offerings, Benny*!" he repeated. "You ask the people to give, but you never tell them to expect a harvest. You only tell them to give. When a farmer sows, he does so *expecting* a harvest. When that grain is ripe and ready to harvest, a portion of the seed is planted for the next harvest, and the balance is used to provide for his needs."

From his comfortable chair, Dr. Roberts began a loving conversation with me, which revolutionized my perspective on giving. He said, "This morning when you asked the people to give, you told them what the Bible said about giving. You shared some wonderful scriptures and challenged them to give, but you didn't tell them to expect to receive. Sowing and reaping go together. I've never known a farmer who planted seed without expecting to reap a harvest."

Genesis 26:12 (KJV) states, "Then Isaac sowed in that land, and received in the same year a hundredfold: and the LORD blessed him." Isaac sowed and received a hundredfold harvest in the same year.

One of the key verses about giving which Dr. Roberts shared with me that morning in my office was Luke 6:38 (KJV) which states, "Give, and it shall be given unto you; good measure, pressed down, and shaken together, and running over, shall men give into your bosom. For with the same measure that ye mete withal it shall be measured to you again."

Now interestingly enough, you are probably aware as I am that the context for this passage is forgiveness:

Therefore be merciful, just as your Father also is merciful. Judge not, and you shall not be judged. Condemn not, and you shall not be condemned. Forgive, and you will be forgiven. Give, and it will be given to you: good measure, pressed down, shaken together, and running over will be put into your bosom. For with the same measure that you use, it will be measured back to you. (Luke 6:36–38)

Even though the *direct* context has to do with forgiveness, the law Jesus referred to is the law of sowing and reaping, which is *universal.*

Dr. Roberts carefully pointed out to me that while giving is referred to once, the blessing that comes from the act of giving is referred to seven times:

1. it shall be given
2. unto you
3. good measure
4. pressed down
5. shaken together
6. running over
7. shall men give into your bosom.

He also showed me that according to this verse when we give, the harvest is so great that it cannot be contained in our hand. It is good measure, pressed down and shaken together to make room for even more, running over, and given into our bosom. The blessings that come to us as a result of giving are so abundant that it takes both arms stretched as far as they can reach to grasp the harvest and carry it home.

As I thought about this, I could imagine men and women walking slowly along, unable to see over the massive load being carried by their outstretched arms and balanced against their chests.

Dr. Roberts went on to explain to me that we should expect a harvest so that we can give again and again. And that the ability to give and give again is the true essence of God's blessing. When we are blessed, when our needs are met, when there is no lack, we are able to give to the Lord's work.

Dr. Roberts summed it up in this way: he told me every time I give to:

• write down the expected harvest.

• thank God for the harvest.

• expect to receive.

• keep giving until the harvest comes—for when it does, I'll be able to give even more.

And that was exactly what I began to do. At that point in my life I longed to be out of debt, for I knew that I could do more for the work of the Lord if I was debt free. I began to ask the Lord in prayer to bring me out of debt, and from that point on I began to include that request in my prayer time.

Each Sunday morning as I prepared to receive the Lord's tithes and offerings at our church, it was customary for me to take five or ten minutes and teach the people what the Bible says about finances and His ability to bless us and meet our needs. While I was sharing the Word of God on the Sunday following Dr. Roberts's visit, these words came to mind: "Write down the expected harvest." As I finished sharing the Word with the people concerning the Lord's tithes and offerings and I prepared my own offering, I quickly turned the offering envelope over and wrote, "Lord, please get me out of debt. In Jesus' name, Amen."

The next Sunday I did the same thing. On the reverse side of my offering envelope I wrote the same words, "Lord, please get me out of debt. In Jesus' name, Amen." Week after week I did the same thing. Each time I participated in an offering, I wrote those same words on the back of my envelope.

One day as I was writing those words on the back of my envelope, the Lord said to me, "Do you really believe what you are writing?"

Startled, I paused for a moment. I glanced down at the words and responded, "Yes, Lord, I believe You can bring me out of debt."

"Then begin to thank Me," the Lord said.

"But how can I thank You when I'm still in debt?" I asked.

The Lord responded, "Begin to thank Me now."

So I prepared my offering in the same way, but I wrote on the back of the envelope: "Thank You, Lord, for bringing me out of debt. Amen." That Sunday as the usher extended the offering bucket toward me to receive the Lord's tithes and offerings, I placed my envelope in the offering bucket and said aloud, "Thank You for bringing me out of debt. Amen." I glanced up quickly to see what reaction there might be from the people. A few curious people looked in my direction, but that was all.

Soon I gained the courage to explain to my congregation what I was doing. And to my surprise, they all began doing the same. They began writing the harvest they were expecting on the back of their offering envelopes. And as the offering containers were passed down the rows, I noticed that some individuals were actually thanking God audibly as they placed their offering envelopes in the offering bucket.

Although there had been no visible answer to my prayer, I continued to write down the harvest I expected and to thank the Lord for my harvest. Each week I could feel more and more expectation rising in my heart. I *knew* the Lord was going to answer my prayer.

A few months later, my wife and I were invited to join a man and his wife for dinner. We enjoyed a lovely time of fellowship around the table that evening. After we had finished our dinner, the man became serious.

"Pastor Benny," he began, "the Lord has been dealing with my wife and me for several months about doing something." He paused a moment and reached into his pocket, from which he produced two envelopes. Then he continued, "I have two envelopes here. One is for you and Suzanne, and the other is for the church. The Lord has been dealing with us, and we must obey Him. This envelope is for you and Suzanne."

I reached out to accept the envelope from the man as I thanked him. He placed it in my hand and stepped back slightly. In the past when someone had presented an envelope to me, stating that it was just for me, it usually contained a small monetary gift. In fact, as I accepted the envelope, my mind went back to a similar situation where someone had given me an envelope "just for me." When I opened it, it contained four dollars!

With that in mind, I started to slip the envelope in my pocket. The gentleman stepped forward again and said, "Open it, Pastor Benny."

Reluctantly, I opened the envelope as the man and his wife looked on. Their faces were quite serious, and they were watching my every move. I reached inside the envelope and pulled out a check. I looked down at the check. I blinked my eyes and looked again. I couldn't believe my eyes! I quickly looked up at the man and his wife and asked, "What is this for?"

"It's for you, Pastor Benny."

"But this is a check for a substantial amount!" I said. "What is this for?"

The man took a step forward and said, "God spoke to my wife and me and told us to pay off your debts. Is that enough?"

By that time both Suzanne and I were crying. We were shocked and thrilled at the same time.

"Is that enough, Pastor Benny?"

"I . . . I don't know," I said through my tears. "I . . .

well . . . I think so." My wife and I did not have many bills, but we did want to be totally out of debt.

Then the man held out another envelope toward me and said, "This envelope is for the church."

I could hardly see through my tears of joy, and I was shaking with excitement. I finally got the second envelope open and reached in to produce the contents. It was a check for even more than the first check! I could hardly believe it! In a moment's time I was out of debt, and the church was blessed!

Later that evening I thought about the incredible sequence of events that had transpired, and as I looked at the check in my hand, I realized that I had just experienced what Dr. Roberts had taught me regarding the law of sowing and reaping. I had written down the expected harvest; I thanked God for my harvest; I expected to receive it; and I had! Not that there is anything magical about this formula. This story isn't about the sequence of events. It's about a God of love who always gives and whom we can never outgive.

When it was time to receive the tithes and offerings in our church the following Sunday, I had so much to share with my congregation. I reminded them of all the times they had seen me write on the back of my offering envelope and heard me say, "Thank You for bringing me out of debt. Amen." And as you can imagine, my congregation filled with praise to God as I said, "I stand before you today out of debt!" And through that, the Lord taught me much about His law of sowing and reaping. And through that, I learned that you cannot outgive God. Now Suzanne and I are able to give much more to the work of the Lord because of His blessings, and this is what God wants for you. Remember, He said to Abraham, "I will bless you and make you a blessing." The Lord wants to bless you so that you can be a blessing to the world, helping in the spreading of the gospel to the ends of the earth.

Give from a Heart of Love

When we read the apostle Paul's words in 2 Corinthians 9:7 that the Lord loves a "cheerful giver," we know that the last thing He would ever want would be for us to give grudgingly or of necessity. When it comes to our children, sometimes they obey us because they know they will be punished if they don't. Although we're glad that our children obey us, we don't derive much pleasure in forced and reluctant obedience. No, we want our children to understand and appreciate our love for them to such an extent that they obey *because they love us.* That they obey not just because they have some sense that it will be better for them, but also because they know that we will be heartbroken if they don't. This is the cheerful kind of giving the Scriptures enjoin.

Now some people try to turn this truth on its head and ask whether we should give at all if we can't give cheerfully. But their question misses the whole point—and the whole blessing. People who can't give cheerfully need to immerse themselves in the Word of God, comprehend the love from which giving stems, and repent (change their minds) so that they *can* experience the blessing of cheerful giving.

The Method He Calls For: The Three Areas of Giving

The Bible outlines three specific areas of giving: tithes, offerings, and alms. All three are essential aspects of giving, yet each serves a different purpose. In the next chapters we will look at each method of giving in more detail.

1. The Tithe (A Debt We're Privileged to Owe)

When I give the Lord His tithe, it is an expression of my love and surrender to Him. *Tithe* basically means "10 percent" and represents the first and best of all I have, indicating that everything else belongs to Him as well. The tithe is given to the place where you are spiritually fed.

2. The Offering (A Seed We're Privileged to Sow)

When I give an offering to the work of the Lord, it is beyond the first tenth (the tithe) and represents a sacrifice and service to Him. An offering is usually given on a freewill basis and can be donated to any special endeavor dedicated to spreading the good news of the gospel.

3. The Alm (A Gift We're Privileged to Let Go)

When mentioning alms, God's Word refers to lending to the poor. Alms are most often intended to assist poor and helpless people. When I give alms, I do so in addition to giving my tithes and offerings. Perhaps you have responded to a special appeal to help needy or underprivileged people through your local church. When you gave that special gift, you were giving alms.

My friends, the Bible has much to say about tithes, offerings, and alms, and in the next few chapters we're going to explore the mind and heart of God in these areas in great depth. As you see the consistent and unwavering teaching of the Scripture from Genesis to Revelation on the Father's desire to bless, I know that like me, you will be motivated to please the Lord as never before in the area of giving.

The Principle of the Tithe Before Moses

They were everywhere! On my right, on my left, towering high above me, shelf after shelf, I was surrounded by toys. And they were not just toys. Before my eyes were the most incredible replicas of automobiles I had ever seen!

Visiting a toy store was not entirely foreign to me, for I had been to this store and others in the past with my wife. But today was different. Today I was exploring a whole new world—toys for boys.

You see, in the past my wife and I had naturally visited the aisles that displayed all the lovely things little girls like. Whether it was Jessica's birthday or Natasha's birthday or simply a day we wanted to make special for them, we always came to the girls' section.

Today, however, I wanted to buy something special for my son, Joshua. He was nearly three years of age, and I wanted to select something just for him. The toys *were* amazing, but what really brought joy to my heart was the prospect of selecting and giving a gift to my precious son.

Upon entering the store, I quickly scanned the directory and then headed in the direction that seemed to contain items appropriate for boys. I walked up and down one aisle, then the next. Finally, I came to a most amazing section: radio-operated cars.

I was surprised to see how many styles and sizes were available. Some were elaborate and detailed, while others were more sleek and stylized. As I studied the choices, I noticed that there was also quite a variety of prices: some were much more expensive than others, but I didn't care, for I was going to buy Joshua the most special car I could find, and price was not my main concern.

I took my time in making my selection, eventually settling on a beautiful red car that I knew he would enjoy playing with. I purchased it, hurried out to my car, and drove home. I drove as fast as the law would allow, for I was eager to present the beautiful toy to him and see the joy on his face.

When I got home, I carried the bag inside and went to find Joshua. I said, "Look, Joshi, look what Daddy got for you."

"What is it?" he asked as he reached out and accepted my gift.

"It's something special for you just because I love you, son," I responded. The box containing the car was rather large, and I had to help him open it. Once the car was out of the box, he looked quizzically at it.

"Do you like it, Joshi?"

He nodded quickly as he continued to stare at the car, now sitting on the floor. It was obvious that he still didn't know quite what to make of his present.

I said, "Let Daddy show you how it works, okay?" I reached for the control box to see if the batteries were in place. "Okay, Joshi, watch the car!" I said, and with that the beautiful red car began to move as I navigated its course from the control box.

Joshua's face absolutely lit up with excitement as he saw the car drive away, then back up, and drive in another direction. And I was thrilled by his response, for I had been so eager to see his reaction to his gift. As a father, I get much pleasure from giving my children pleasure—there is absolutely nothing quite like it.

After several minutes, I placed the remote control device in Joshua's little hand and helped him move the control lever. Together we moved the lever back and forth, watching as the car drove through the house. To a spectator, it may have been difficult to determine who was having a more enjoyable time: Joshua or me!

We had a special time together that afternoon, spending some very special time together as we laughed and watched the car motor its way from room to room in our house. Oh, the joy that we parents have in our ongoing and ever-deepening relationship with our children!

Our Heavenly Father

I'm so grateful that our relationship with God is an ongoing one, that He takes us literally "from glory to glory." And how glorious it is to be in an ever-deepening love relationship with our wonderful heavenly Father! Every day as I spend more time with the blessed Master in the Word of God and in prayer, I become that much more acquainted with His ways, that much more familiar with what is important to Him, that much more motivated to please Him in every way.

And as I become more and more acquainted with His Word, His will, and His ways, I become ever more convinced of the importance of tithing in our lives. Yet I sometimes talk to people—sincere, convinced brothers and sisters in the Lord—who say, "Tithing is part of the Old Testament law and not a requirement for believers today." Frankly, I cringe when I hear that. I fear that these good people are experiencing giving only as a requirement or *demand* when our heavenly Father wants us to experience it as a *delight*. No one requires us to give to someone we love—it happens naturally. It is delightful to give to those who have given to us first—and we experience this delight when we tithe.

But not only can people who interpret the Bible this way miss the joy, they also miss the fact that the very principle of the tithe was introduced with Adam, and Abraham tithed to Melchizedek. And so I want you to see in this chapter that from the very dawn of history, our heavenly Father has given us the best, and people who love Him give Him the best.

The word tithe refers to a tenth or a tenth part of something. So when I'm talking about tithing, I'm talking about the privilege and practice of giving 10 percent of our income to the work of the Lord.

Adam and the Tithe (Gen. 2)

Genesis 2 is a very familiar passage of Scripture, but have you ever stopped to really think about how wonderful the world was that the Father prepared for Adam? The Garden of Eden was wonderful far beyond description. What a blessing it was to him, to live, work, rest, play, and pray in such a beautiful place! But not only was it beautiful, it was as big as the entire Middle East! (Gen. 2:11–14) And it was his to enjoy—more than he needed, more than he could use, it was a lavish gift of love to him.

The Father endowed Adam with a magnificent mind capable of marvelous creativity and capacity such that he could name and remember the animals. And he had a body free from the experiences of age, disease, and death.

He enjoyed rich fellowship with the Father, who delighted in Adam so much that He loved walking with him in the cool of the day. Oh, how rich those times must have been! No other created being had known the kind of fellowship with the Father that Adam was privileged to experience.

The Father loved Adam so much that He anticipated Adam's need for help and companionship and created Eve. For even in the midst of the beauty of Eden and the wonder of close communion with the Father, it was still not good for Adam to dwell alone.

God cared for him in every way, and in the midst of their fellowship, God surrounded Adam with wealth, excellence, and magnificence. I love how Moses described just one element of its wonder: "And the gold of that land is good." (Gen. 2:12) Get the picture? Not just gold—*good* gold!

God gave Adam the wonderful garden to enjoy. Yet in the midst of all that God had given him, He warned Adam that one thing in the paradise was not his—the tree of the knowledge of good and evil:

> Then the LORD God took the man and put him in the garden of Eden to tend and keep it. And the LORD God commanded the man, saying, "Of every tree of the garden you may freely eat; but of the tree of the knowledge of good and evil you shall not eat, for in the day that you eat of it you shall surely die." (Gen. 2:15–17)

In God's setting apart the tree of the knowledge of good and evil, I believe that God established the principle of the tithe. Think about it for a moment: Adam was never forbidden to eat of the tree of life or anything else in the garden. So why would a God who had lavished such luxury on Adam forbid him to eat from the fruit of the tree of the knowledge of good and evil? I'm convinced that the Father did this so that Adam would have an opportunity to demonstrate his love for God through *obedience*. What I'm about to teach you now is *very* important.

You and I cannot receive what is ours in Christ apart from obedience, and in establishing this law, the Father gave Adam a chance to obey. In great love, it's as if our heavenly Father was saying to Adam, "I love you, and this magnificent garden is yours to enjoy. But I want your love back, and the way you can show Me that you love Me is through obedience, *so don't touch that tree.*"

In that sense, the tree of the knowledge of good and evil was set apart to God—it demonstrates the principle of *tithe* to God. In a similar way today, I express my love to God when I give Him what is His (the tithe) and don't touch it by holding onto it for myself. What a privilege to bring joy to the heart of our wonderful heavenly Father!

Cain and Abel and the Tithe (Gen. 4)

So God established the principle of the tithe with Adam, and Adam in turn taught it to Cain and Abel, for the Scripture declares:

> Now Adam knew Eve his wife, and she conceived and bore Cain, and said, "I have acquired a man from the LORD." Then she bore again, this time his brother Abel. Now Abel was a keeper of sheep, but Cain was a tiller of the ground. And in the process of time it came to pass that Cain brought an offering of the fruit of the ground to the LORD. Abel also brought of the firstborn of his flock and of their fat. And the LORD respected Abel and his offering, but He did not respect Cain and his offering. And Cain was very angry, and his countenance fell. (Gen. 4:1–5)

I love this insight from R. T. Kendall:

> Tithing in any case does more for us spiritually than it does at any material level. There is no doubt about this. It releases the Spirit. It taps other resources in our inheritance in Christ that otherwise had been shut tight. This is why Adrian Rogers has said, "The purpose of tithing is to prove God," for tithing is "His way to *develop faith* in Him." Dr. Rogers tells the story of a man who made his sons work in the cornfields while other

boys were out in the swimming hole, playing in the fields, and doing other things. Someone remonstrated with the man and said, "Why do you make those boys work so hard in your cornfields? You don't need all that corn." The man answered: "Sir, I'm not raising corn, I'm raising boys."[1]

God does not use the tithe to raise money, as if He had need of any; He uses it to raise children. In the Garden of Eden God used the principle of the tithe to teach Adam obedience through setting apart things wholly unto the Lord. The Father also revealed the tithe to Adam's children for the same purpose, and they brought offerings unto the Lord.

Yet God accepted Abel's offering while He rejected Cain's. Why would that be so? Some say Cain's sacrifice was unacceptable because the fruit of the earth had been cursed. I don't believe this is an adequate explanation; for after all, the entire created universe was under curse. Others say that Abel offered his sacrifice in faith while Cain did not, and certainly, this is part of it, for the Scriptures state, "By faith Abel offered to God a more excellent sacrifice than Cain, through which he obtained witness that he was righteous, God testifying of his gifts; and through it he being dead still speaks." (Heb. 11:4)

But I believe that there is still more within this tragic account. Although it is true that "without faith it is impossible to please [God]" (Heb. 11:6), it is also true that faith without love is empty: "Though I have all faith, so that I could remove mountains, but have not love, I am nothing. And though I bestow all my goods to feed the poor, and though I give my body to be burned, but have not love, it profits me nothing." (1 Cor. 13:2–3) I believe that the Father peered into Cain's heart and detected only the blackness of jealousy and obligation. From the very beginning of time, God has wanted us to give Him our hearts first, then our tithes. Nowhere is this expressed more magnificently than by David:

> The sacrifices of God are a broken spirit,
> A broken and a contrite heart—
> These, O God, You will not despise." (Ps. 51:17)

Our precious heavenly Father has always looked at the heart. That enabled Him to describe David as "a man after God's own heart" even though he had committed terrible sins. Yet when it came to the Pharisees in the New Testament, whose hearts were not right with God, the Lord Jesus saw through their showiness and self-righteousness:

> Then, in the hearing of all the people, He said to His disciples, "Beware of the scribes, who desire to go around in long robes, love greetings in the marketplaces, the best seats in the synagogues, and the best places at feasts, who devour widows' houses, and for a pretense make long prayers. These will receive greater condemnation."

But in connection to a certain widow, the Word of God tells us that Christ looked up:

> and saw the rich putting their gifts into the treasury, and He saw also a certain poor widow putting in two mites. So He said, "Truly I say to you that this poor widow has put in more than all; for all these out of their abundance have put in offerings for God, but she out of her poverty put in all the livelihood that she had."
> (Luke 20:45–21:4)

While the Pharisees and the rich made a great show of their religiosity and their giving, it was the *heart* of this poor widow that moved the Lord. Our gifts to God are to no avail unless they are birthed in the warmth of the Spirit's love.

Abraham & Melchizedek and the Tithe (Gen. 14)

Genesis 14 is the first time *tithing* is explicitly mentioned in the Scripture. There we are told of the victory Abraham won over the heathen kings, and where we are also told of the appearance of Melchizedek, the priest of the most high God, who when meeting Abraham declared, "And blessed be the most high God, which hath delivered thine enemies into thy hand. And he [Abram] gave him [Melchizedek] tithes of all." (Gen. 14:20 KJV) Abraham (then known as Abram), the father of the nation of Israel and the man through whom the entire world has been blessed, presented tithes to the mysterious Melchizedek.

This act of gratitude took place more than four hundred years before God wrote the Ten Commandments on tablets of stone on Mount Sinai—before the Mosaic Law or old covenant. Tithing began as an act of worship when Abraham recognized God as the most high God, Possessor of heaven and earth, and Deliverer from all his enemies.

Before we look at Genesis 14, you may be wondering how Abraham knew to offer tithes to Melchizedek. I believe that it was a revelation of the blessed Holy Spirit, just as it was with Adam. I'm sure he had learned to tithe when he was still young.

Years before the battle depicted in Genesis 14, God called Abraham from Ur of the Chaldees (in modern-day Iraq) to the land of Canaan. The words of the Scripture are magnificent in their understatement:

> Now the Lord had said to Abram:
> "Get out of your country,
> From your family
> And from your father's house,
> To a land that I will show you.

I will make you a great nation;
I will bless you And make your name great;
And you shall be a blessing.
I will bless those who bless you,
And I will curse him who curses you;
And in you all the families of the earth shall be blessed." So Abram departed as the Lord had spoken to him, and Lot went with him. And Abram was seventy-five years old when he departed from Haran. (Gen. 12:1–4)

At the age of seventy five, with his wife, household, and nephew in tow, "Abram departed as the Lord had spoken to him" on a journey of hundreds of miles to a place he had never been, such was his childlike confidence in a loving God. The writer of Hebrews painted a dramatic picture:

By faith Abraham obeyed when he was called to go out to the place which he would receive as an inheritance. *And he went out, not knowing where he was going.* By faith he dwelt in the land of promise as in a foreign country, dwelling in tents with Isaac and Jacob, the heirs with him of the same promise; for he waited for the city which has foundations, whose builder and maker is God. (Heb. 11:8–10, emphasis added)

Oh, what great faith Abraham had in God! And our heavenly Father always comes through—not somehow but triumphantly, for we read that God blessed Abraham greatly in the land of promise with livestock, silver, in gold. (Gen. 13:2) The blessing of the Father *made* Abraham rich, and the blessing of the Father *kept* Abraham rich. When the wealth of Abraham and his nephew Lot became so great that the land couldn't contain their holdings, Abraham said to Lot:

"Please let there be no strife between you and me, and between my herdsmen and your herdsmen; for we are brethren. Is not the whole land before you? Please separate from me. If you take the left, then I will go to the right; or, if you go to the right, then I will go to the left." . . . Then Lot chose for himself all the plain of Jordan, and Lot journeyed east. And they separated from each other. . . . And the Lord said to Abram, after Lot had separated from him: "Lift your eyes now and look from the place where you are—northward, southward, eastward, and westward; for all the land which you see I give to you and your descendants forever. And I will make your descendants as the dust of the earth; so that if a man could number the dust of the earth, then your descendants also could be numbered. Arise, walk in the land through its length and its width, for I give it to you." (Gen. 13:8–17)

Oh, how pleased God was to see Abraham's dependence on Him by choosing to stay where God had placed him.

Shortly thereafter, several kings in that area conspired together to invade Sodom and Gomorrah. They defeated Sodom and Gomorrah, and seized Lot and his possessions. On hearing the news, Abraham had not a moment's hesitation. He mustered his 318 servants and immediately went after the invading forces. In a spectacular nighttime victory, Abraham and his men routed the enemy, chasing them beyond Damascus and recovering the people and possessions. (Gen. 14:14–16)

An army of just 318 men armed with the mighty power of God went out and decisively defeated the thousands who had routed Sodom and Gomorrah. In fact, Abraham pursued the armies all the way from Bethel to north of Damascus—about as far as the distance between Los Angeles and San Francisco. Just think of these 318 men, on foot or on horseback, going all that way, fighting vastly superior forces, decisively defeating them, and then returning with the captives and spoils in tow. Only God almighty can bring about a victory like that.

Yet Abraham's battle was really just beginning, for on returning from battle he was confronted by two kings who couldn't have been more different from each other in who they were, what they offered—and what they wanted. Notice that the first of the two kings to meet Abraham was the king of Sodom: "And the king of Sodom went out to meet him at the Valley of Shaveh (that is, the King's Valley), after his return from the defeat of Chedorlaomer and the kings who were with him." (Gen. 14:17) The very word *Sodom*, represents evil in all its wickedness. The evil king of the evil city met Abraham first, trying to steal his victory.

God had given Abraham the victory. God was Abraham's source of prosperity—he didn't need anything from anybody as long as the Lord was on his side. And he certainly didn't need anything at all from the wicked king of a city so wicked that except for Lot, his wife, and their daughters, it would soon be entirely destroyed. (Gen. 19)

But Abraham, great man of faith that he was, ignored the king of Sodom, that emissary of satan, for before him came one of the most remarkable beings recorded in the Scripture, the priest-king Melchizedek: "Then Melchizedek king of Salem brought out bread and wine; he was the priest of God Most High." (Gen. 14:18)

Virtually everything we know about Melchizedek is found in Psalm 110 and Hebrews 5–7. So remarkable was Melchizedek that Jesus is likened to him, for the Scriptures declare:

Where the forerunner has entered for us, even Jesus, having become High Priest forever according to the order of Melchizedek. For this Melchizedek, king of Salem, priest of the Most High God, who met Abraham returning from the slaughter of the kings and blessed him, to whom also Abraham gave a tenth part of all, first being translated "king of righteousness," and then also king of Salem, meaning "king of peace," without father, without mother, without genealogy, having neither beginning of days nor end of life, but made like the Son of God, remains a priest continually." (Heb. 6:20–7:3)

To a famished group of warriors, a gift of bread and wine would be quite fitting in and of itself. But priest-king Melchizedek is a type of Christ, and bread and wine represent the body and blood of our blessed Savior, so I believe that it is a mistake to view this gift merely as a meal. No, Melchizedek nourished Abraham *spiritually* with a foretaste of Christ as well as blessed him:

And [Melchizedek] blessed [Abraham] and said:
"Blessed be Abram of God Most High,
Possessor of heaven and earth;
And blessed be God Most High,
Who has delivered your enemies into your hand."
(Gen. 14:19–20)

Abraham's response was immediate: "And he gave him a tithe of all." (Gen. 14:20) Tithing ought *always* to occur if you are nourished spiritually.

Now satan had tried to steal the victory once, but Abraham would not be sidetracked. But neither does satan give up easily. Through the king of Sodom, he came after Abraham again, hissing to Abraham, "Give me the persons, and take the goods for yourself." (Gen. 14:21) On the face it, the king of Sodom's offer was much more enticing than that of Melchizedek, for while Melchizedek offered sustenance, the king of Sodom offered loot. Melchizedek offered blessing and true prosperity—the king of Sodom offered stuff, and stuff that wasn't his to give anyway, for Abraham had the power, not the king of Sodom.

This is always how satan works. He sets before us something that might look good, but satan never delivers what he promises. And satan doesn't have the authority: *We* have the authority!

Once again, Abraham would have nothing of satan's deceiving schemes. But Abraham said to the king of Sodom, "I have raised my hand to the LORD, God Most High, the Possessor of heaven and earth, that I will take nothing, from a thread to a sandal strap, and that I will not take anything that is yours, lest you should say, 'I have made Abram rich.'" (Gen. 14:22–23)

He refused the king's offer by saying that he would not even take a shoestring from the spoils, for then no one could take the credit for having made Abraham rich except the Lord God. Abraham's faith and trust were in God and he expected to receive his riches from God alone. When he went to deliver Lot, he expected to receive and to be blessed, but not from the hand of man—only from the hand of God almighty.

Oh, my friend, it is so important that we learn from Abraham. To experience the true biblical prosperity that the Father so earnestly desires for us, we must never forget four vital principles:

First, *God is our victory. He* prospers us and gives us the power to prosper.

Second, satan *will* try to steal our victory. And he won't just try once; he will try repeatedly.

Third, what satan offers us may look better than what God offers us, but satan *always* lies—he never comes through, except as he *robs, kills, and destroys.*

Fourth, tithing is our appropriate and automatic response whenever we are nourished spiritually— *always.*

So you see, tithing isn't about law or grace, Old Testament or New Testament—it's about love, it's about obedience, and it's about the Father's intention to raise obedient children. And as such, giving in general and tithing in particular are taught from the beginning of God's Word clear through to the end.

CHAPTER 8

Tithing in the Old and New Covenants

The apostle Paul declared, in 2 Timothy 3:16, 17, " *All* Scripture is given by inspiration of God, and is profitable for doctrine, for reproof, for correction, for instruction in righteousness, that the man of God may be complete, thoroughly equipped for every good work." Although there are sixty-six books of the Bible, written by many people over hundreds of years, they in fact form *one* Book with *one* Author—God almighty. And in this one Book we find the mind and heart of the Lord revealed to us.

From cover to cover, we see the Father's great desire to prosper His children. From cover to cover, we see how He delights when His children obey Him. And so from cover to cover, we see the importance that the Lord places on His people tithing. In the previous chapter we saw how tithing has been a part of man's walk with God from Adam onward. In this chapter, I want to show you what the Bible reveals about tithing in the old covenant, which came through Moses, and the new covenant, which came through the Lord Jesus.

The psalmist proclaimed, "Bless the LORD, O my soul,/ And forget not all His benefits." (Ps. 103:2) We've already seen the prosperity that God delights to shower on those who are obedient to Him, but tithing brings such great blessings into our lives that I can't help but testify to them again to make sure that you're ready to receive this wonderful teaching from the Word of God.

Tithing and Spiritual Growth It's true that the Lord uses our tithes to support His work. And with the unprecedented outpouring of revival taking place around the world, more money than ever before is needed to take advantage of the amazing opportunities opening up for evangelism, missions, church planting, and discipleship. But it is also true that God the Father has ordained tithing at least in part because of the wonderful things that happen to us when we tithe. As R. T. Kendall notes:

> Apart from the fact that were all Christians to tithe it would solve the church's financial problems, I am sure that becoming a tither provides a definite breakthrough for every Christian. It unlocks the door of his mind, heart, and will. It releases. It emancipates. It frees. Becoming a tither is a milestone in a Christian's life.
>
> In other words, tithing does something for you *spiritually*. You will only ask, "Why did I not start tithing sooner?" It does something for you that cannot be explained in terms of material return. It sets you on a course to become more than you have been—more what God wants you to be, more of what you are naturally capable of being. Tithing is so essential to your development as a Christian that nothing will be its adequate substitute.[1]

Kendall's testimony is the experience of every mighty child of God throughout the ages. Consider, for instance, the experience of George Muller, who testified:

I have been for fifty years, by God's grace, acting on the principle of Christian giving according to the Scriptures, and I cannot tell you the abundance of spiritual blessing I have received to my own soul through acting thus; that is, seeking to be a cheerful giver; seeking to give as God has been pleased to prosper me. Many beloved saints are depriving themselves of wondrous spiritual blessing by not giving as stewards of what is entrusted to them . . . depriving themselves of vast spiritual blessings, because they have not followed the principles of giving systematically, and giving as God prospers them, and according to a plan . . . habitually giving on principles, just as God enables them.[2]

Tithing and Stress

All of us are trying to get more out of life. And there are two ways to do this. The first is to try to stretch and squeeze more into our lives. We try to get by on less sleep, do two or three things at once, have the latest equipment so that we can be most productive, and so on. Now don't get me wrong. There is nothing wrong with any of this. But the net effect of it all is to produce great stress in our lives as we try to go fast enough to keep up with *more* while at the same time having *less* physical and emotional energy available.

But there is another way. The Word of God sets before us a way of living that says that *less is more*. This other way is the way of obedience. The Lord says, if you'll give to Me one day in seven, your life will be more productive than if you try to go at full tilt seven days a week. Your land will be more productive if you rest it regularly than if you plant it year after year after year. Your income will go farther if you tithe it to Me than if you consume all of it upon yourself. In other words, God's principles are the way to escape the rat race the Lord never intended for you.

Along these lines, financial expert Bruce Howard makes this fascinating observation:

When I do tax preparation, I often ask my clients: "What are the top five stress points in your life?" People who say they are stressed out over their finances are convinced they can't afford to tithe. In contrast, I have found that people who tithe their income don't list financial pressures as one of their top stressors. . . . In Malachi, the Lord says, "Test me in this [in the matter of tithing], and see if I will not throw open the floodgates of heaven and pour out so much blessing that you will not have room enough for it." That blessing is not always material; I think it's a sense of contentment.[3]

Truly, little *is* much when God is in it!

Tithing: The Mind and Heart of God

It is often said that generally, the Old Testament reveals the *mind* of God while the New Testament reveals the *heart* of God. But we musn't take this too far. After all, no one can read a passage like Hosea 11 and say they have not seen the heart of God and His amazing, loyal love. While on the other hand, you cannot read the masterful logic of the book of Romans and say that you have not encountered the stunning brilliance of the mind of God. But because the Old Testament is about three times longer than the New Testament, *as a general rule* we find more detail on the Lord's thinking in the Old Testament. This is particularly true in regard to tithing.

We're going to look, first at the Old Testament, then at the New Testament, to see what they reveal about tithing. My purpose is not to give you an encyclopedic, exhaustive, and *exhausting* treatment of the biblical testimony on tithing. Instead, I want to highlight the major points and, in so doing, motivate you to experience the blessing of biblical tithing.

The Mind of God (Tithing in the Old Covenant)

What Is the Tithe?

When we speak about tithing in the Law of Moses, we need to recognize that there were actually three tithes.

The first, or general, tithe is described in Leviticus 27:30–33:

> And all the tithe of the land, whether of the seed of the land or of the fruit of the tree, is the LORD's. It is holy to the LORD. If a man wants at all to redeem any of his tithes, he shall add one-fifth to it. And concerning the tithe of the herd or the flock, of whatever passes under the rod, the tenth one shall be holy to the Lord. He shall not inquire whether it is good or bad, nor shall he exchange it; and if he exchanges it at all, then both it and the one exchanged for it shall be holy; it shall not be redeemed.

The second tithe is described in Deuteronomy 14:22–27:

> You shall truly tithe all the increase of your grain that the field produces year by year. And you shall eat before the LORD your God, in the place where He chooses to make His name abide, the tithe of your grain and your new wine and your oil, of the firstborn of your herds and your flocks, that you may learn to fear the LORD your God always. But if the journey is too long for you, so that you are not able to carry the tithe, or if the place where the LORD your God chooses to put His name is too far from you, when the LORD your God has blessed you, then you shall exchange it for money, take the money in your hand, and go to the place which the LORD your God chooses. And you shall spend that money for whatever your heart desires: for oxen or

sheep, for wine or similar drink, for whatever your heart desires; you shall eat there before the LORD your God, and you shall rejoice, you and your household. You shall not forsake the Levite who is within your gates, for he has no part nor inheritance with you.

The third tithe is described in Deuteronomy 14:28–29:

At the end of every third year you shall bring out the tithe of your produce of that year and store it up within your gates. And the Levite, because he has no portion nor inheritance with you, and the stranger and the fatherless and the widow who are within your gates, may come and eat and be satisfied, that the LORD your God may bless you in all the work of your hand which you do.

What Does the Tithe Teach Us About the Mind of God?

1. God wants our first and our best. He will not accept anything less. In fact, the person who tried to substitute something less was required to give *both* the second best and the best. (Lev. 27:33) As we'll explore in Chapter 10 when we study the book of Malachi, anyone who tried to offer the Lord something other than the first and the best was under a curse.

One way or another, the Lord gets our first and our best. We either cooperate with Him and so experience the blessing, or resist Him and lose the blessing—as well as the best. R. T. Kendall notes:

W. A. Criswell tells us the story about the pastor who was asked, "How many church members do you have?" The answer was, "One hundred fifty." The pastor was further asked, "How many of them are tithers?" The pastor replied, "One hundred fifty." In astonishment the inquirer exclaimed, "What! All one hundred fifty, the entire church, are tithers?" "Yes indeed," said the pastor. "About fifty of them bring the tithe into the storehouse, and God collects it from the rest."[4]

Now an implication of the fact that God wants the first and the best is that we are to base our tithe on all of our income—not just that which remains after taxes and other things are taken out. And as you examine the passages above, you can clearly see that when God wants the first, He means the *first*, not a portion from what remains. Again, R. T. Kendall has the last word: "To narrow the basis of the tithe to the 'net' is to undermine the promise of God's blessing, for to tithe only the 'net' borders on giving grudgingly and may well militate against the promise of blessing. It is as though you really do not believe you cannot out-give the Lord."[5]

2. God wants more than 10 percent. A *tithe*, as you know, means "a tenth". But with the three tithes mentioned above, His people ended up giving much more than 10 percent. As theologian Charles Ryrie observes, "Thus the proportion was clearly specified and every Israelite was obligated to bring to the Lord approximately 22 percent of his yearly income."[6]

3. God wants his servants supported. The Lord declared in Numbers 18:21, "Behold, I have given the children of Levi all the tithes in Israel as an inheritance in return for the work which they perform, the work of the tabernacle of meeting." God intended that the tithe should support His ministers and His work.

I want to ask you a very direct question here: Is your church paying your pastors as much as it should? My heart is sad when I hear about pastors who are paid pathetically or who even have to work at another job to make ends meet. I tell you quite plainly *this should not be*! Your pastors deserve "double honor"—and should not drive beat-up cars, live in ramshackle houses, or wear threadbare clothes. I don't mean that ministers should live like princes or potentates, but neither should they live like paupers.

4. God wants His ministers to tithe. Numbers 18:26 states, "Speak thus to the Levites, and say to them: 'When you take from the children of Israel the tithes which I have given you from them as your inheritance, *then you shall offer up a heave offering of it to the Lord, a tenth of the tithe.*' " They were to tithe from their income to the Lord's work.

5. God wants us to support the poor. The third tithe, which was given every third year, was explicitly intended to support the poor, the alien, and the unfortunate. When we give to the Lord, we give to support His work and His servants—yet integral to both must be the support of the poor.

6. God wants us to celebrate when we give. This important principle is easily overlooked. Tithing wasn't just writing a check and going home. The second tithe was designed to be a time of rejoicing—a party to celebrate the Father's faithfulness.

After the harvest, the people journeyed to Jerusalem with their tithes, following the Lord's command to "spend that money for whatever your heart desires: for oxen or sheep, for wine or similar drink, for whatever your heart desires; you shall eat there before the LORD your God, and you shall rejoice, you and your household." (Deut. 14:26) They celebrated in the presence of the Lord, remembering and rejoicing in His care, demonstrating to all that He "satisfies your desires with good things so that your youth is renewed like the eagle's." (Ps. 103:5 NIV)

7. God wants us to ask for a blessing when we give. The Father wants to bless us, and when we're obedient, it is perfectly acceptable to ask Him for His blessing—in fact, He commands us to. God declares in Deuteronomy 26:12–15 (NIV):

When you have finished setting aside a tenth of all your produce in the third year, the year of the tithe, you shall give it to the Levite, the alien, the fatherless and the widow, so that they may eat in your towns and be satisfied. Then say to the LORD your God: "I have removed from my house the sacred portion and have given it to the Levite, the alien, the fatherless and the widow, according to all you commanded. I have not turned aside from your commands nor have I forgotten any of them. I have not eaten any of the sacred portion while I was in mourning, nor have I removed any of it while I was unclean, nor have I offered any of it to the dead. I have obeyed the LORD my God; I have done everything you commanded me. *Look down from heaven, your holy dwelling place, and bless your people Israel and the land you have given us as you promised on oath to our forefathers, a land flowing with milk and honey.*"

Notice that in the presence of the Lord, they were to recount their obedience. Then after having solemnly reported to the Lord their full obedience, they were *commanded* to ask for a blessing. My friend, there is nothing at all unseemly or presumptuous about asking the Lord to bless you—provided that you've been obedient.

The Heart of God (Tithing in the New Testament)

Jesus and the Tithe

A great portion of the Old Testament discusses the tithe and God's requirement of it from the nation of Israel. By comparison, the New Testament does not say as much about the topic. But we must remember it is the Word of God whether old or new. From Genesis to Revelation, it *is* His Word. Some will say that the tithe is not binding on believers in the church age, for they say it's Old Testament, it's Law. But the facts are that the tithe started before the law of Moses. God ordained it in the very beginning, starting with Adam, as we have already seen. Tithing is neither new nor old—it is the Word of God always present. It is always in the now as God's Word is in the now. The Lord Jesus Himself showed us that the tithe was still intact in the New Testament.

The first thing I want you to notice is the Lord's declaration in Matthew 5:17, "Do not think that I came to destroy the Law or the Prophets. I did not come to destroy but to fulfill."

The second thing I want you to notice is the Savior's command in Matthew 22:21 to "render therefore to Caesar the things that are Caesar's, and to God the things that are God's." If there is anything in the Scriptures that is clearly declared to be God's, it is the tithe.

The third thing I want you to notice is that nested in the Savior's condemnation of the Pharisees is approval of their practice of tithing. The Lord declares in Matthew 23:23–28: "Woe to you, scribes and Pharisees, hypocrites! For you pay tithe of mint and anise and cummin, and have neglected the weightier matters of the law: justice and mercy and faith. *These you ought to have done*, without leaving the others undone." (Matt. 23:23, emphasis added) He didn't condemn them for tithing; He condemned them for not obeying the Law in other matters. Jesus wanted them to do *both*.

From this, I am convinced that tithing is the privilege and responsibility of every New Testament Christian. But a benefit that we have today is that we have a new power available to us as we obey the Lord in the area of tithing.

What Is Grace Giving?

One of the most refreshing and central truths of the whole New Testament is that we are no longer under law but under grace. The apostle Paul asserted:

> There is therefore now no condemnation to those who are in Christ Jesus, who do not walk according to the flesh, but according to the Spirit. For the law of the Spirit of life in Christ Jesus has made me free from the

law of sin and death. *For what the law could not do in that it was weak through the flesh, God did by sending His own Son in the likeness of sinful flesh, on account of sin: He condemned sin in the flesh, that the righteous requirement of the law might be fulfilled in us who do not walk according to the flesh but according to the Spirit.* (Rom. 8:1–4, emphasis added)

The Law told us what to do, but it didn't give us the power to fulfill it. But because of the sacrifice of the Lord Jesus, the Holy Spirit dwells within those of us who trust Him. And now we have the power to do what He wants us to do—more than that, "in all these things we are more than *conquerors* through Him who loved us." (Rom. 8:37)

Not only do we have the Holy Spirit dwelling inside us to give us the power as we obey, but we are constantly reminded of and overwhelmed by the love of God. When we experience that love, we respond with love and gratitude, which manifest themselves in obedience. Here is a story that illustrates the difference in motivation between law and love.

The story is told of a woman who was married to a tyrant of a man for thirty years. Each day before her husband left for work, he gave her a written list of duties that he expected her to complete before his return in the evening. She cowered in silence each day as he hurled the daily duty roster in her direction before marching out the front door.

Throughout the day, she constantly checked the list, fearful that she might inadvertently overlook one of his orders. And by the time he returned home each evening, she was exhausted from the tension and fear as she struggled to complete her assignments.

Each evening, he went over the checklist point by point to be certain that nothing had gone unattended. Then he gulped down his evening meal, retired to his favorite chair, and fell asleep until bedtime.

After thirty years of marriage, her husband became ill and eventually died from the illness. The widow lived alone for several years. Then she met a man who treated her with the utmost respect and was very kind and considerate. They grew to love each other and were eventually married.

The newlyweds decided to live in the home the woman owned. There they lived their later years together and enjoyed a wonderful relationship. He treated her like a queen, and she enjoyed a very happy life with him.

One day as she sat down on the couch in their living room, she slid her hand along the side of the cushion to straighten it. She felt something protruding from beneath it. She stood up and lifted the cushion, curious to see what her hand had touched. She pulled out a wrinkled piece of paper, unfolded the paper, and glanced at its contents. As she read the words on the paper, a small tear escaped from the corner of her eye and trickled down her face.

In her hand she held an old tattered piece of paper with familiar handwriting on it: a handwritten list of orders prepared by her former husband who had passed away. Seeing that list again almost made her shudder in fear, for it reminded her of a totally different life from what she now lived. She read over the words on the paper, line by line, as tears of joy began to slowly flow down her cheeks, caressing her mature face and then falling on the paper she held in her hand.

As her eyes moved to the top of that old torn checklist once again, a tiny smile appeared on her face. She realized that she was doing everything that was on that list and much more. But there was a difference. In the past she had nervously completed the duties on the list out of fear; now she was doing everything contained on the list and much more because of a loving relationship.

She crumpled up the old tattered paper and walked over to the garbage can. "I do all this and more now," she said to herself as she threw the paper in the trash, ". . . and without a list!''

You see, love *transforms* us. When Roy Harthern talked to me about the law of tithing, I began to give out of obedience. But when I began to realize God's great love for me and His desire to bless me, I was overwhelmed with the new insight, and everything became different. I experienced the Father's love. I obeyed Him in giving because I loved Him, and I experienced His blessing of love. When I fell in love with the Lord, tithing was no longer an issue.

Now for all of these reasons, if anything we should be giving more than a tithe in the new covenant. Tithing is not the *destination* here in the age of grace—it is the departure point!

What Does This Teach Us About the Heart of God?

1. God wants us to become givers and be generous in our giving as He is—not only in tithes and offerings, but in all areas:

> Give to him who asks you, and from him who wants to borrow from you do not turn away. (Matt. 5:42)

> Give to everyone who asks of you. And from him who takes away your goods do not ask them back. (Luke 6:30)

> Heal the sick, cleanse the lepers, raise the dead, cast out demons. Freely you have received, freely give. (Matt. 10:8)

2. God wants us to give faithfully:

> Let a man so consider us, as servants of Christ and stewards of the mysteries of God. Moreover it is required in stewards that one be found faithful. (1 Cor. 4:1–2)

3. God wants us to give secretly:

Take heed that you do not do your charitable deeds before men, to be seen by them. Otherwise you have no reward from your Father in heaven. Therefore, when you do a charitable deed, do not sound a trumpet before you as the hypocrites do in the synagogues and in the streets, that they may have glory from men. Assuredly, I say to you, they have their reward. But when you do a charitable deed, do not let your left hand know what your right hand is doing, that your charitable deed may be in secret; and your Father who sees in secret will Himself reward you openly. (Matt. 6:1–4)

4. God wants us to give freely:

For if there is first a willing mind, it is accepted according to what one has, and not according to what he does not have. (2 Cor. 8:12)

5. God wants us to give regularly:

Now concerning the collection for the saints, as I have given orders to the churches of Galatia, so you must do also: On the first day of the week let each one of you lay something aside, storing up as he may prosper, that there be no collections when I come. (1 Cor.1 6:1–2)

6. God wants us to give cheerfully:

So let each one give as he purposes in his heart, not grudgingly or of necessity; for God loves a cheerful giver. (2 Cor. 9:7)

Many people who truly want to understand the Lord's will in the matter of giving wonder whether they should give at all if they are unable to give cheerfully. This question deserves a thoughtful answer. I know of no better answer than that given by R. T. Kendall, so I'm going to quote it for you at length:

> It is likewise stated by some that if you are tithing, you are not giving "cheerfully." This is of course a reference to Paul's words in 2 Corinthians 9:7. . . . Do people who take this line think that Paul would want you to bring the amount of your giving down to a level low enough for you to be able to give "cheerfully"? This same would apply to the amount of time spent in prayer. And yet sometimes I do not feel "cheerful" when I pray. Does this mean I should not pray? When I prefer to sleep instead of praying, should I sleep because I can do this more cheerfully? . . .
>
> The same principle applies to the command, "Husbands, love your wives, even as Christ also loved the church, and gave himself for it." (Eph. 5:25) Why do you suppose Paul said that? Because sometimes we don't "feel" love toward our wives as a spontaneous emotion. But we love them none the less. We love by showing. By doing. Not feeling. But doing. This is the theme that runs right through the New Testament. There are times we feel a certain emotion and this may be based on our own mood or temperament or external circumstances. Other times we don't feel the same emotion. As for giving cheerfully, Paul added: "And God is able to make all grace abound toward you; that ye, always having all sufficiency in all things, may abound to every good work." (2 Cor. 9:8) Why do you suppose Paul added those words? Because he wanted to *motivate* these Corinthians to give cheerfully. For giving cheerfully is *not* what comes very naturally and it frequently is *not* the way we are going to feel when a thousand and one

needs compete for our pay check. . . . The result of doing what I ought to do—whether praying, giving, or disciplining my own feelings so that I demonstrate love—is that I am *so glad* I did what I knew I should do. . . . Tithing is no different.[7]

Tithing is God's will, and as such, it is a choice privilege and an amazing opportunity. And because of this, we would do well to heed Roger Babson's slightly humorous and completely insightful advice: "More people should learn to tell their dollars where to go instead of asking them where they went."[8]

Offerings and Alms in the Old and New Testaments

*Hear the story from God's Word
That kings and priests and prophets heard.
There would be a sacrifice
And blood would flow to pay sin's price.*

*Precious Lamb of Glory, Love's most wondrous story.
Heart of God's redemption of man.
I worship the Lamb of Glory.*

*On the cross God loved the world
While all the powers of hell were hurled.
No one there could understand
The One they saw was Christ the Lamb.*

*Precious Lamb of Glory, Love's most wondrous story.
Heart of God's redemption of man.
Glory to the Lamb. Pure as snow I stand,
Worshipping the Lamb of Glory.*[1]

The Privilege of Great Giving

What can we say in the face of such great love? That the Father would choose to love us even while we were His enemies; that He would send His precious, sinless Son to die on the cross and in our place when we couldn't have cared less; that we could be reconciled to Him, forgiven, sanctified, adopted as His children, filled with joy, blessed, prospered—what do we say in the face of such great love? Our hearts fill to overflowing in praise and adoration. We want to do everything for Him, everything we can to bring pleasure to His heart. He has paid so much to allow us to have relationship with Him that we want to do everything we can to deepen it—and that means obedience in every area, including the area of giving.

We have seen that the Lord commands us to tithe, for fundamentally the tithe is *His.* In love He has promised that the moment we do this, He will open the floodgates of heaven and prosper us beyond all that we can imagine.

But tithing is just one of the privileges He gives us. The Scriptures speak of giving to the Lord beyond the Tithe. And as we give to the Lord *beyond* the tithe, in love we experience even more of the Father's abundance. You see, when we give God the tithe, we give Him what is already His. But when we give *beyond* the tithe, we offer to Him sacrificially. In fact, sometimes in the Old Testament, offerings are referred to as "sacrifices." The tithe, however, could never be called a sacrifice, for it belongs to God already.

When I tithe, I acknowledge that He is the Lord of my life. I honor the Lord with my substance. I show to all that I recognize Him as almighty God, the King of kings and Lord of lords. But when I give to Him over and above the tithe, I tangibly lavish praise and worship upon Him.

When I tithe, I not only acknowledge that He is Lord of my life, I confess Him to be Lord over all—the One who is the owner of everything—and by contrast, I am a stranger and a pilgrim in this land. And when I give to Him over and above the tithe, I show also that I love Him so much that I want Him to have my all.

When I give the Lord His tithe, I show that I recognize His ownership, His lordship, and His authority. But when I give an offering to God, I do it in recognition of the fact that He sacrificially gave because of His love and now I give because of my love.

Make no mistake about it. The tithe brings great blessings. But what father isn't moved by a child who goes over and above for their father just because she loves him? Any father would lavish even greater affection on that kind of child, wouldn't he?

Now we're going to look at some special kinds of giving found in the Old and New Testaments that are over and above the tithe. And again I want to reiterate that my purpose is not to give you an encyclopedic, exhaustive, and *exhausting* treatment of the biblical testimony on offerings and alms. Instead, I want to emphasize some key areas and, in so doing, motivate you to experience the blessing of biblical giving.

Giving to the Poor

If there is among you a poor man of your brethren, within any of the gates in your land which the LORD your God is giving you, you shall not harden your heart nor shut your hand from your poor brother, but you shall open your hand wide to him and willingly lend him sufficient for his need, whatever he needs. . . . You shall surely give to him, and your heart should not be grieved when you give to him, *because for this thing the LORD your God will bless you in all your works and in all to which you put your hand.* For the poor will never cease from the land; therefore I command you, saying, "You shall open your hand wide to your brother, to your poor and your needy, in your land." (Deut. 15:7–8, 10–11, emphasis added)

He who has pity on the poor lends to *the Lord*, And *He will pay back what he has given.*" (Prov. 19:17, emphasis added)

He who gives to the poor will not lack,
But he who hides his eyes will have many curses. (Prov. 28:27, emphasis added)

Do not fear, little flock, for it is your Father's good pleasure to give you the kingdom. *Sell what you have and give alms; provide yourselves money bags which do not grow old, a treasure in the heavens that does not fail, where no thief approaches nor moth destroys.* For where your treasure is, there your heart will be also. (Luke 12:32–34, emphasis added)

These passages clearly indicate that the Lord wants us to give to relieve the needs of the poor. And just like the Lord in each of these passages where He calls us to be generous to the poor, the Lord promises to bless us in return.

For example, in Psalm 41 we find seven blessings promised to those who consider the poor. The Word of God declares in verse 1: "Blessed is he who considers the poor;/ *The Lord will deliver him in time of trouble.*" Here we find the first promise: it is for deliverance if we consider the poor.

Verse 2: "The Lord will *preserve* him and *keep* him *alive,*/ And he will be *blessed* on the earth;/You will *not deliver him to the will of his enemies.*" Second, the Lord will preserve us. Third, in the same verse, the Lord promises to keep us alive, meaning long life. Fourth, the Lord promises we will be blessed upon the earth; we will have no lack and will experience true biblical prosperity. Fifth, we will not be delivered to the will of our enemies.

Verse 3: "The Lord will *strengthen* him on his bed of illness;/You will *sustain* him on his sickbed." Sixth, the Lord promises to strengthen us in times of weakness. Seventh, God promises healing in times of sickness.

Thus, the Lord makes seven amazing promises to those who give to the poor:

1. Deliverance
2. Preservation
3. Longevity
4. Prosperity
5. Protection
6. Strength
7. Healing

Giving to Special Projects

The Lord is doing so much in the world today, and He is using men and women of great faith to perform daring exploits for Him. But ambitious plans usually require significant funds. As you are involved in the work of the Lord, you will become aware of special opportunities to advance His work through strategic giving.

The tabernacle of the Lord, as described in the Old Testament, was magnificent to behold. God called on Moses to construct it, and Moses called on the people to give the materials and expertise necessary to build it, as the Scriptures declare in Exodus 35:21–24:

Then everyone came whose heart was stirred, and everyone whose spirit was willing, and they brought the Lord's offering for the work of the tabernacle of meeting, for all its service, and for the holy garments. They came, both men and women, as many as had a willing heart, and brought earrings and nose rings, rings and necklaces, all jewelry of gold, that is, every man who made an offering of gold to the Lord. And every man, with whom was found blue, purple, and scarlet thread, fine linen, and goats' hair, red skins of rams, and badger skins, brought them. Everyone who offered an offering of silver or bronze brought the LORD's offering. And everyone with whom was found acacia wood for any work of the service, brought it.

But here is the amazing part—the power of God had so captured these people that *they had to be restrained from giving more.* The Word declares, "So Moses gave a commandment, and they caused it to be proclaimed throughout the camp, saying, 'Let neither man nor woman do any more work for the offering of the sanctuary.' And the people were restrained from bringing, for the material they had was sufficient for all the work to be done—*indeed too much.*" (Ex. 36:6–7)

I believe we're going to see the day again when God's people will give to God's work in such a way that ministries and pastors will say as Moses did, we have enough! Remember, God almighty gave the wealth of the Egyptians to Israel, and the Bible declares in Exodus 12:36 that they spoiled the Egyptians.

Now, why did God give the wealth of the Egyptians to Israel? Was it so that they could go shopping in the wilderness? Was it so that they could build houses in the desert? No! It was so that they could build His tabernacle. In fact, even when they entered the promised land, the Word of God declares they inhabited homes they did not build. Why? Because the Word of God declares in Proverbs 13:22 (KJV) that "a good man leaveth an inheritance to his children's children: and the wealth of the sinner is laid up for the just."

Again, we in the church are about to see this promise come to pass in our day so that the kingdom of God can be built in the lives of men and women and the gospel preached to the ends of the earth. And notice, God gave them the wealth of the Egyptians *before* they left Egypt. And I believe the wealth of the sinner will be placed in our hands, also, just before we leave this "Egypt," the world.

Giving to Those Who Feed You

"Let him who is taught the word share in all good things with him who teaches." That was the instruction of the apostle Paul in Galatians 6:6. I personally believe that we need to tithe through the local church. Yet the Lord has raised up many fine ministries that teach the Word through television, radio, print, on-line services, and meetings. The Word of the Lord is clear—if you are being taught through them, you have a responsibility to support them.

But not only a responsibility, a privilege as well. As the apostle Paul was thanking the Philippians for their continued financial support for him, he noted that their gift was "a sweet-smelling aroma, an acceptable sacrifice, well pleasing to God." (4:18) And because of their obedience to the Word of God, the apostle Paul told the Philippians that "my God shall supply all your need *according to His riches in glory* by Christ Jesus." (4:19) I'll say it again—no matter how hard we try, we cannot outgive God!

Giving and Integrity

Thomas Brooks had it right when he said, "Saving grace makes a man as willing to leave his lusts as a slave is willing to leave his galley, or a prisoner his dungeon, or a thief his bolts, or a beggar his rags." When the grace of God touches us, when the Spirit of God takes residence in our lives, when the sacrifice of the Son of God becomes real to us, sacrificial giving to those in need becomes natural—yes, even inevitable. As the passages below indicate, where there is no giving, there is no authenticity, no reality.

The Word of God says we are to share our bread with the hungry, bring the poor to our homes, cover the naked, and not hide ourselves from individuals in need, and then the Lord promises:

> Then your light shall break forth like the morning,
> Your healing shall spring forth speedily,
> And your righteousness shall go before you;
> The glory of the LORD shall be your rear guard.
> Then you shall call, and the LORD will answer;
> You shall cry, and He will say, "Here I am." (Isa. 58:8–9)

The Word of God further declares that at Christ's coming, all nations will be gathered before Him:

> He will separate them one from another, as a shepherd divides his sheep from the goats. And He will set the sheep on His right hand, but the goats on the left. Then the King will say to those on His right hand, "Come, you blessed of My Father, inherit the kingdom prepared for you from the foundation of the world: for I was hungry and you gave Me food; I was thirsty and you gave Me drink; I was a stranger and you took Me in; I was naked and you clothed Me; I was sick and you visited Me; I was in prison and you came to Me." (Matt. 25:32–36)

I will never forget when I met Mother Teresa in New York in 1995. She looked at me, lifted her hand, showing me all five fingers, and said, "When you help the poor, just look at your hand, and remember." And then she went on to count how many fingers she had.

ONE   TWO   THREE   FOUR   FIVE
"YOU   DID   IT   TO   ME"

Jim Poynter took me to my first Kathryn Kuhlman service, and he is one of my dearest friends. He and I were riding in a car back in the seventies when he illustrated this principle for me with a parable that I will never forget. A woman received a call on her telephone one day at about 9:00 in the morning. It was Jesus. He announced to her that at 3:00 that afternoon He would be visiting her house. Of course, she was very excited by the news and immediately threw herself into cleaning up the house and making it as presentable as possible for the Master. After all, He was coming that very afternoon.

An hour or two later, as she was cleaning the house, there was a knock at the door. It was a little orphan boy, who said, "Oh, please, ma'am, could you give me some food? I haven't eaten for days."

"I'm sorry, little boy, but I'm much too busy to help you. You see, Jesus is coming to my house today at 3:00, and I have to be ready."

Later there was another knock on the door. This time it was an elderly gentleman. It was very cold outside that day, and his clothes were little more than rags—not at all appropriate to the chilly conditions outside.

The man begged the woman, "Please, ma'am, could you give me some spare clothes from your husband's closet? Would you please help me? I'm so very cold."

"You'll have to come back later," the woman replied. "I'm extremely busy right now. Jesus is coming at 3:00, and I simply have to prepare for his arrival."

Later there was yet a third knock at the woman's door. This time it was a young woman carrying a small child. She was a widow. Destitute, she was in desperate need of food, clothing, and shelter on that cold day. She said, "Please, ma'am, my child and I are in such need of food and clothing, and we're so cold out here. Please help us!"

"No, I simply cannot right now. I know you have your problems. But so do I. Jesus is coming to my house at 3:00, and I have no time to do anything other than prepare for His arrival."

Three o'clock soon came, and the house was prepared

for Jesus' arrival. But there was no knock on the door. Instead the phone rang again. It was Jesus. The woman answered and said, "Jesus, why aren't you here? Everything was prepared for Your arrival."

But the Master answered, "I've come three times already and you sent Me away, rejecting Me each time."

My friend, never forget that when the poor come to you, it is really the Lord Jesus—and you must treat them as you would Him.

I'll never forget the time a pastor-friend of mine named Don told me in tears a most remarkable account that also illustrates this passage. On Easter Sunday many years ago, my friend Don was having dinner with a group of ministers at a restaurant. Suddenly, an older man entered the restaurant. He was ragged looking, and his apparel was not at all appropriate for Easter Sunday when everyone was wearing the very best. The waitress threw the man out of the restaurant without thinking twice about it, assuming from his appearance that he had no money.

Don saw what was happening, so he called the waitress over and asked her why she had thrown the man out. "Oh," she replied. "Don't think anything about him. He's just a bum."

Don asked the waitress, "Well, if I pay for his lunch, would you let him back in?"

"Sure," she replied indifferently.

Don found the man still outside the restaurant. "Please, sir, come back in and eat. I'm paying for your lunch."

"You don't have to do that," the older man replied.

"Oh, yes, I do. I'm a minister. I'm a Christian. It's Easter, and I *want* to feed you. Come on," Don replied.

So Don brought the man back into the restaurant, sat him down at a table, and made sure that his order was taken. Then Don went back to his table and his lunch with his friends.

Don noted that the waitress served the man his meal,

and then Don returned to concentrating on his friends and the conversation they were having. A few minutes later, he glanced over at the table where the man was sitting, only to find that he had disappeared.

Confused, Don went over to the waitress and said, "Ma'am, I told you I would pay for his meal. Why did you throw him out again?"

"I didn't," she replied. "I don't know where he is."

Don and the other ministers searched the restaurant for him. They looked in the men's room. They looked outside in the parking lot. They looked everywhere in the immediate vicinity around the restaurant, but the man was nowhere to be found. They were all greatly puzzled. The man had disappeared without a trace, and he hadn't even touched his food. The napkin, the water, the silverware, none of it had even been moved.

Eventually, they finished their meal and returned to their homes. That evening Don was praying. Suddenly, he had the unmistakable sensation that somebody was in the room. He turned around, and there before him was the same man he had seen at the restaurant that afternoon— same outfit, same beard, same everything—it was the same man.

Fixing eyes with Don, the older man said, "I was hungry—and you fed me," and disappeared into thin air. From that point on, Don's life was never to be the same again. He was transformed, and God began to bless him and his family in a most remarkable way.

"Inasmuch as you've done it unto the least of these, My brethren, you've done it unto Me." (Matt 25:40)

Giving and Glory (the Macedonian Example)

Yes, biblical giving blesses others. Yes, biblical giving blesses us. But never lose sight of the fact that biblical giving results in thanksgiving to God, as the apostle Paul noted in 2 Corinthians 9:10–15, where he declares:

Now may He who supplies seed to the sower, and bread for food, supply and multiply the seed you have sown and increase the fruits of your righteousness, while you are enriched in everything for all liberality, which causes thanksgiving through us to God. For the administration of this service not only supplies the needs of the saints, but also is abounding through many thanksgivings to God, while, through the proof of this ministry, they glorify God for the obedience of your confession to the gospel of Christ, and for your liberal sharing with them and all men, and by their prayer for you, who long for you because of the exceeding grace of God in you. Thanks be to God for His indescribable gift!

When people experience biblical giving, their hearts well up with thanksgiving to God. And as more and more people are obedient in their giving, the glory of the Lord grows and grows and grows.

Oh, my friend, His hands are blessing hands—and how He delights to reward the sacrificial faithfulness of His children. John Bunyan, that towering giant of the faith, described in a simple couplet so well the life of blessing that is available to you and me if we would but obey Him:

There once was a man,
Some called him mad;
The more he gave,
The more he had.

Malachi—The Burden of the Lord

One of the things I have tried so hard to emphasize in this book is the love of our heavenly Father for His children. And that the easiest way to understand and then triumphantly live the Christian life is to fall in love with the Lord—to let Him love you and then respond to His love with obedience. The benefits and blessings of this kind of love relationship are far beyond description.

God is committed to getting you on the biblical road to blessing. After all, He has sacrificed so much already for you to enter in, as the apostle Paul declares in Romans 8:32, "He who did not spare His own Son, but delivered Him up for us all, how shall He not with Him also freely give us all things?"

Never forget the Lord's commitment to get each of us on the biblical road to blessing. Yet sometimes we so resolutely resist getting on the biblical road to blessing that God is *forced* to discipline us so that we will stop hurting ourselves and cheating ourselves out of the abundance He wants to bestow on us.

No parent likes to discipline their children. In fact most of us hate it. However, corrective, positive discipline is sometimes *the only* loving course, as the writer of the book of Hebrews persuasively explained:

And you have forgotten the exhortation which speaks to you as to sons:
"My son, do not despise the chastening of the Lord,
Nor be discouraged when you are rebuked by Him;
For whom the LORD loves He chastens,
And scourges every son whom He receives."
If you endure chastening, God deals with you as with sons; for what son is there whom a father does not chasten? But if you are without chastening, of which all have become partakers, then you are illegitimate and not sons. Furthermore, we have had human fathers who corrected us, and we paid them respect. Shall we not much more readily be in subjection to the Father of spirits and live? For they indeed for a few days chastened us as seemed best to them, but He for our profit, that we may be partakers of His holiness. Now no chastening seems to be joyful for the present, but painful; nevertheless, afterward it yields the peaceable fruit of righteousness to those who have been trained by it. (Heb. 12:5–11)

The book of Malachi, the last book in the Old Testament, is the heart cry of an exasperated Father to His wayward children. The people of Israel had failed to take seriously the principles and practices of giving that we've explored in the previous chapters. God is trying to get through to His rebellious and confused children.

Because of this there is some tough language in the book—powerful and provocative—just as there would be if someone transcribed one of your "woodshed" conversations with one of your children. But even though the language is hard, the tender heart of the Father still comes through. In fact, the basic message of the book of Malachi is this: "I want to bless you, but I *can't* when you disobey Me."

In our study together on giving, I have highlighted the tender aspect of the Father's love and the promises He holds out to faithful givers. In this chapter we will look at the tough aspect of the Father's love—the chastening we invite when we fail to take seriously the Father's commands in the area of giving. But like so much of Scripture, the message of the Lord in the book of Malachi becomes clear only when we examine it as a whole.

Malachi Chapter 1

The Father's Burden

The burden of the word of the Lord to Israel by Malachi. (v. 1)

Every parent aches inside when they see their child making hurtful choices, and the Lord is no different. Throughout its history, the nation of Israel veered from the way of obedience and blessing described in Deuteronomy 28. But the people's behavior served not to make the Lord angry (although He was angry) so much as to make Him sad. God wanted the best for His children—He wanted them to make the right choices. That desire weighed so heavily on His heart and the words were so strong that they constituted "the *burden* of the word of the LORD to Israel." The words were heavy on His heart and He wanted to talk to Israel because He cared so much for them. God knew that they were heading for disaster if they didn't change. And so He came to them with His burden.

I Love You

"I have loved you," says the Lord.
"Yet you say, 'In what way have You loved us?'" (v. 2)

Never lose sight of the fact that the book of Malachi begins with a statement of love. So many people jump right into chapter 3 with its talk about robbing God or being cursed—or chapter 4 that ends, as it does, with a curse that they miss the heart of love running through this book and providing the context for words that in isolation could seem harsh.

When we correct our children, the first thing we usually do is try to establish that we love them and that our discipline is flowing from a heart of love. In the book of Malachi, God did the same. But as you can see from Israel's reply, they were so out of fellowship with the Lord that they weren't even aware of all the manifestations of love they were receiving from Him. And so in blind anger Israel spit back, "In what way have You loved us?"

God's answer was pithy and penetrating: "I loved you by choosing you."

> "Was not Esau Jacob's brother?"
> Says the LORD.
> "Yet Jacob I have loved;
> But Esau I have hated,
> And laid waste his mountains and his heritage
> For the jackals of the wilderness."
> Even though Edom has said,
> "We have been impoverished,
> But we will return and build the desolate places,"
> Thus says the LORD of hosts:
> "They may build, but I will throw down;
> They shall be called the Territory of Wickedness,
> And the people against whom the LORD will have
> indignation forever." (vv. 2–4)

In their waywardness they failed to grasp that all that they had was from the good hand of their gracious God, that *the only thing* that separated them from Esau's fate of futility was *God's choice*. The Lord didn't love Jacob because he was more lovable than Esau, He loved Jacob because of His sovereign choice. So God grabbed them by the shoulders and tried to shake them into understanding, "The only reason you're not experiencing My wrath right now is that I've chosen not to punish you. If you were Esau, you'd be *toast.*"

I Want You to Honor Me

> "A son honors his father,
> And a servant his master.
> If then I am the Father,
> Where is My honor?
> And if I am a Master,
> Where is My reverence?
> Says the LORD of hosts
> To you priests who despise My name.
> Yet you say, 'In what way have we despised Your name?'
> You offer defiled food on My altar.
> But say,
> 'In what way have we defiled You?'
> By saying,
> 'The table of the LORD is contemptible.'
> And when you offer the blind as a sacrifice,
> Is it not evil?
> And when you offer the lame and sick,
> Is it not evil?
> Offer it then to your governor!
> Would he be pleased with you?
> Would he accept you favorably?"
> Says the LORD of hosts. (vv. 6–8)

In this passage we can almost picture the Father grabbing Israel by the shoulders and saying, "Wake up son! I love you. I want to be your friend. I'm not your enemy. I want to bless and build you, *but I can't* when you disobey Me like this. I cannot stand idly by when you insult Me by giving

Me what is lame and blind and torn and unacceptable. Don't pretend you're giving when you're really just throwing things away and using My house as a Dumpster."

Almighty God expects His children to honor Him because He is our Father; to respect Him because He is our Master. When we try to give things to the Lord that we would never have the nerve to give a government official or other powerful person, we show Him how lightly we regard Him.

The Lord wants our *first* and He wants our *best*. Now listen to me carefully—*anything less insults Him*. Even more significant, it brings a curse, for the Lord declared:

> "When you bring injured, crippled or diseased animals and offer them as sacrifices, should I accept them from your hands?" says the LORD. *Cursed* is the cheat who has an acceptable male in his flock and vows to give it, but then sacrifices a blemished animal to the Lord. For I am a great king," says the LORD Almighty, "and my name is to be feared among the nations." (Mal. 1:13–14 NIV)

I want to share with you now a deep spiritual truth. Suppose a person decides to give $1,000 to a secular charity and then $100 to their church. Is that giving God the best? No, and as a result, the $1,000 that could have been an investment for eternity is now cursed. The person's best was the $1,000, and we should *always* give the Lord our best. And because of the curse, *it would have been better for the person not to have given at all.*

Better not only for the person, but for the organization as well. I think R. T. Kendall is absolutely right when he observes:

> Charitable organizations should be sustained by either non-Christians or Christians who have first given *all* their tithes to the church—and then to that organiza-

tion. That organization moreover will be much better off and is far more likely to have God's blessing if it is not sustained by funds that belonged to the Lord. I do not doubt that a charitable organization not connected to the church can be blessed of God. This matter comes under the category of God's "common grace". But any organization that receives funds that ought to have gone to the church will be impoverished, not enriched. If the church got what it ought to *have* the whole world would be better off and worthy non-ecclesiastical organizations would be more blessed than ever. Funds that ought to be the Lord's that go elsewhere militate against God's blessing in the world generally and everyone loses.[1]

The promise of Proverbs 3:9–10 is still the same today,

Honor the LORD with your possessions,
And with the firstfruits of all your increase;
So your barns will be filled with plenty,
And your vats will overflow with new wine.

I Want You To Pray

"But now entreat God's favor,
That He may be gracious to us. . . .
For from the rising of the sun, even to its going down,
My name shall be great among the Gentiles;
In every place incense shall be offered to My name,
And a pure offering;
For My name shall be great among the nations,"
Says the LORD of hosts. . . .
"For I am a great King,"
Says the LORD of hosts,

"And My name is to be feared among the nations."
(vv. 9, 11, 14)

Even if, like the nation of Israel, you haven't given God
your first and your best, through prayer and repentance *today* can be your day for breakthrough and a fresh start. With
all that the nation of Israel had done to offend the Lord, He
still called upon them to begin doing what was right and
surrounding it with prayer.

You see, a tithe without prayer will not yield the harvest
that it might have otherwise. That was why He commanded
the nation of Israel to "return" to Him in Malachi 3 *before*
talking to them about the tithe. The tithe offered without
the heart being right with God is not accepted. It is no
different from a religious practice.

To be sure, the law of sowing and reaping still applies,
but the anointing of the Lord will be missing—His mighty,
manifest presence that brings a superabundant harvest.
This kind of harvest comes only in the midst of relationship.

Malachi 2   In chapter 1, the Lord told Israel that He
wanted to bless them but could not as long as
they failed to honor Him and failed to pray. In
chapter 2, the Lord sternly warned the children of Israel
whom He loved. Most of the Father's words in chapter 2
were directed toward the priests. Yet there is also an important warning in them for us, for today believers in the Lord
are "a chosen generation, a royal priesthood, a holy nation,
His own special people, that you may proclaim the praises of
Him who called you out of darkness into His marvelous
light; who once were not a people but are now the people of
God, who had not obtained mercy but now have obtained
mercy." (1 Peter 2:9–10)

When we fail to honor God with the first and the best,
when we fail to bathe our giving in prayer, the Lord curses
our blessings, for Malachi 2:2 declares:

"If you will not hear,
And if you will not take it to heart,
To give glory to My name,"
Says the LORD of hosts,
"I will send a curse upon you,
And I will curse your blessings.
Yes, I have cursed them already,
Because you do not take it to heart."

The Lord cursed their blessings, not only by making their offerings fruitless, but also by publicly humiliating them, just as they had humiliated the Lord with their pathetic offerings. The language that Malachi used was intentionally graphic to capture their attention:

"Behold, I will rebuke your descendants
And spread refuse on your faces,
The refuse of your solemn feasts;
And one will take you away with it.
Then you shall know that I have sent this
commandment to you." (vv. 3–4)

In the Middle East where I spent my childhood, there is no greater insult than to take dung and spread it on someone's face. The Father's response demonstrates just how insulting it is to Him when we fail to honor Him by giving Him our first and our best.

Malachi 3 *His Presence*

"Behold, I send My messenger,
And he will prepare the way before Me.
And the Lord, whom you seek,
Will suddenly come to His temple,
Even the Messenger of the covenant,
In whom you delight.

Behold, He is coming,"
Says the LORD of hosts.
"But who can endure the day of His coming?
And who can stand when He appears?
For He is like a refiner's fire
And like launderer's soap.
He will sit as a refiner and a purifier of silver;
He will purify the sons of Levi,
And purge them as gold and silver,
That they may offer to the LORD
An offering in righteousness.
Then the offering of Judah and Jerusalem
Will be pleasant to the LORD,
As in the days of old,
As in former years." (vv. 1–4)

In chapter 3, the most amazing transformation took place. In chapter 1, the Lord said their offerings were polluted. Yet in the first portion of chapter 3, He said that their offerings would become pure when the Messiah came. Jesus made all the difference!

Now the first three verses are prophetic, having in mind the first and second comings of the Lord Jesus. The church is fulfilling them today, and there will be a prophetic fulfillment for the nation of Israel as a whole when they accept Jesus as their Messiah at His second coming.

When we "put on the Lord Jesus Christ, and make no provision for the flesh, to fulfill its lusts," (Rom. 13:14) He gives us the faith we need to follow through on what we know to be right by giving the Lord our first and our best. His presence becomes so real to us that we envelop our giving as well as everything we do in vital prayer to the Father.

His Love

> *For I am the* LORD, I do not change;
>   Therefore you are not consumed, O sons of Jacob.
> (v. 6, emphasis added)

This verse is the preface to one of the most significant passages in the Scripture on the subject of giving, which makes it crucial to understand. We can't fully appreciate the Lord's exhortations about returning to Him and not robbing Him unless we understand this verse.

You see, the Lord sovereignly made a decision to choose the nation of Israel and enter into a covenant with Israel. His decision was based on His own will—not the nation's performance. He made a decision to love Israel, and nothing Israel could do would change that. So even when He had to talk straight to Israel, even when He had to discipline them, it was always motivated by love. And the Father was always waiting with loving arms for them to return in obedience.

Instead of being awestruck by the Father's love, instead of responding to this great love with gratitude and obedience, they took His love for granted, not even realizing that they had done so, for we read in verse 7:

> Yet from the days of your fathers
> You have gone away from My ordinances
> And have not kept them.
> Return to Me, and I will return to you,"
> Says the LORD of hosts.
> "But you said,
> 'In what way shall we return?' "

So again the Lord explained how they were to return, and the blessing that was theirs if they did.

His Promise

> Will a man rob God?
> Yet you have robbed Me!
> But you say,
> "In what way have we robbed You?"
> In tithes and offerings.
> You are cursed with a curse,
> For you have robbed Me,
> Even this whole nation. (vv. 8–9)

Israel was robbing the Lord, not so much by withholding tithes and offerings as by offering to the Lord what was corrupt and unacceptable. The people thought that by holding back the best, they were enriching themselves, but all that they had succeeded in doing was bringing a curse upon themselves.

The Father did not give His Son to die on the cross for His people to end up living under a curse. No, He intended for them to live in a blessing. But those rebellious children couldn't understand that the way to abundance was through giving God the first and the best. So He offered His wayward children a most remarkable proposition:

> Bring all the tithes into the storehouse,
> That there may be food in My house,
> And try Me now in this,"
> Says the LORD of hosts,
> "If I will not open for you the windows of heaven
> And pour out for you such blessing
> That there will not be room enough to receive it.
> And I will rebuke the devourer for your sakes,
> So that he will not destroy the fruit of your ground,
> Nor shall the vine fail to bear fruit for you in the field,"
> Says the LORD of hosts;

"And all nations will call you blessed,
For you will be a delightful land,"
Says the LORD of hosts. (vv 10–12)

In this passage God *commands* us to prove Him. He as
much as says, "I guarantee these results (or double your
money back)!" This bold, one might even respectfully say,
brash, statement by the Lord was designed to get the attention of wayward Israel. Almighty God promised remarkable
blessings for those who obeyed the four elements found in
the phrase, "Bring all the tithes into the storehouse."

The first thing I want you to notice is that the Lord
commanded them to "*bring* all the tithes into the storehouse." He didn't want them to *send* the tithes. He enjoined
them to physically bring tithes into the storehouse. The reason He asked that, I believe, was to make the act of giving
more meaningful. For instance, if I get a gift for my mother,
I don't want to mail it; I want to give it to her myself. If I get
flowers for my wife, I want to hand them to her myself, not
only because it is more meaningful to me but also because it
is more meaningful to *her*. When we *bring* our tithes to the
Lord, we show Him that we love Him.

The second thing I want you to notice is that the Lord
commanded them to "bring *all* the tithes into the storehouse." This verse could be better rendered, "Bring *the
whole* tithe into the storehouse." Now remember in terms of
the context of the book of Malachi, the people of Israel
were guilty of trying to offer crippled and diseased animals
to the Lord. So what God was calling for was not only that
they should *fully* tithe, but also that they should tithe *the first
and the best.*

The third thing I want you to notice is that the Lord
commanded them to "bring all the *tithes* into the storehouse." The test required them to give as the Lord commanded, that is, to pay the tithes they owed Him.

The fourth thing I want you to notice is that the Lord

commanded them to "bring all the tithes into the *store-house,/ That there may be food in My house.*" It is my personal conviction that "My house" referred to His people. In other words, the passage did not refer to food stores in the temple as much as it referred to the church as the living temple, as the apostle Paul explained in 2 Corinthians 6:6, "For we are the temple of the living God. As God has said: 'I will live with them and walk among them, and I will be their God, and they will be my people.' "

This would mean, then, that God's purpose for the tithe is to feed His people. So our tithe brought to God not only will bring blessings to us, it brings blessings to His people because God is then able to feed them and take care of them in order to bless the world with the gospel.

When we meet the four conditions that the Lord has set down for this test, we literally have to brace ourselves for the blessings that follow.

The Tithe and Its Results

There are seven blessings mentioned in Malachi 3 that extend to every area of our lives. It is so important to recognize here that the Lord blesses us spiritually and materially. To ignore one or the other is to sell God short and not be honest with the Scripture. R. T. Kendall says it so well when he observes:

> The blessing at a natural level is inferior to the spiritual blessing. . . . But it cannot be ignored. "I will rebuke the devourer for your sakes, and he shall not destroy the fruits of your ground; neither shall your vine cast her fruit before the time in the field, saith the LORD of hosts." (Mal. 3:11) The "blessing" promised by the prophet (Mal. 3:10) is primarily spiritual, but the fact that the prophet continues as he does indicates that this blessing is *not only* spiritual. God has a way of blessing us materially that just

happens to coincide with our having become tithers. The 90% that we keep to ourselves after the tithe is given to the Lord has a way of equaling the 100% before the tithe. Sometimes the 90% goes far, far beyond what that 100% would have purchased. How can this be? Frankly, I do not know. But I believe it.[2]

Blessing #1: "Open for you the windows of heaven"

The "windows of heaven" refers sometimes to the rain, sometimes to God's miraculous provision of food, but *always* to His presence. When the heavens are shut, the Lord has hidden His presence and withheld His blessing. There is a fascinating passage in the book of Acts where the apostle Peter referred to the Lord Jesus being kept in heaven until the time comes for God to restore everything. But when the heavens are opened and the Savior returns, "times of *refreshing* will come from the Lord." (Acts 3:17–23) Here we see that an open heaven speaks of revival.

Blessing #2: "Pour out for you such blessing That there will not be room enough to receive it"

Pour is an interesting word, for it actually means to "empty out." It gives the idea of a bucket being emptied out upon your life. God is saying, "I'll empty out My bucket of blessings upon your life; I want to give you literally every last drop. What I promised you in Deuteronomy 28 I want to pour out upon you—and then some." And not only that, just think of how this relates to the kinds of prosperity mentioned in the Scripture that we explored in Chapter 5— being showered with contentment, showered with enjoyment, and showered with the fruit of the Spirit, just to name a few.

Blessing #3: "I will rebuke the devourer for your sakes"

The word "rebuke" is a strong word, and refers to throttling someone "through strong admonitions or actions.''[3] I believe that satan, the enemy of our souls, is the devourer referred to here. And thus the word of the Lord is that He will give us a special measure of protection against the attacks of the devil.

Blessing #4: "That he will not destroy the fruit of your ground"

Of course when the Lord spoke these words, most people made their living through farming. Thus protection of "the fruit of your ground" meant that their income and their future were protected. I have met some individuals who have fine jobs and make a lot of money but yet never have enough to pay their bills. I believe that is because the devil is destroying their income and they don't see the result of their labor. But the blessing mentioned here destroys the destroyer!

Blessing #5: "Nor shall the vine fail to bear fruit for you in the field"

This is a continuation of the previous blessing and promises that fruitfulness—the law of sowing and reaping—will prevail. Your labor will be fruitful—hard work will come to fruition. But I also believe that an implication of this passage is that your "fruit" will be protected. God will protect your children. He will keep them safe, and they will have their needs met.

Blessing #6: "And all nations will call you blessed"

The Father's hand of blessing will be so evident in your life that it will be obvious to all that there is something special about you. As a result, you will be a testimony—a living example to all those around you—of the goodness of God.

Blessing #7: "You will be a delightful land"

Now when the Lord refers to "land" here, He is actually referring to the *people* who live in the land. Those whom

God delights in, He chooses for service. So this promise actually refers to the blessing of the Almighty that results in His using those in whom He delights in His service.

- Blessing #1: Revival
- Blessing #2: Abundance
- Blessing #3: The enemy rebuked
- Blessing #4: Fruit protected
- Blessing #5: Family protected
- Blessing #6: Will become a testimony of God's goodness
- Blessing #7: Chosen for service

Malachi 4 Having thrown down the tremendous challenge of chapter 3, in chapter 4, the Lord reminded His chosen people of both the blessing He wanted to be theirs and the judgment He would one day bring on those who failed to heed His warning.

What a time those of us will have who heed the Father's warning and live as obedient children, for the Scripture declares:

"But to you who fear My name
The Sun of Righteousness shall arise
With healing in His wings;
And you shall go out
And grow fat like stall-fed calves.
You shall trample the wicked,
For they shall be ashes under the soles of your feet
On the day that I do this,"
Says the LORD of hosts." (vv. 2–3)

But never forget, God's Word is *true.* His expectation of obedience is real. The stakes are high. So today and everyday, take God at His Word and remember, what He promised He will do. He said to us as His people, "Prove Me now." Let's not forget He is the Lord, and His promises are "yea and amen."

And remember, God's supernatural power will be yours as you act upon His Word. And when you act, you act in the realm of the natural, and God responds in the realm of the supernatural. What an adventure it will be! Remember, heaven responds to actions on earth. And God always responds to actions filled with faith toward Him, for example:

1. Every miracle requires an act on your part. A spiritual miracle requires a spiritual act. When you are born again, you must believe, confess publicly Christ Jesus. That is an act.

2. A physical miracle requires a physical act. When you are healed, you must do something physically. When the Lord saw people who could not walk, He said, "Take up thy bed and walk." That is a physical act.

3. A financial miracle requires a financial act. The Lord declared, "Give, and it shall be given unto you." In the next chapter, we'll be dealing with some very natural and practical applications that will help you get on the biblical road to blessing.

CHAPTER

11

Getting Started on the Biblical Road to Blessing

Whatjoy we have had as we have searched the unfathomable riches of the Word of God! As I study again the amazing love of our heavenly Father for us, my heart leaps in praise to God. When I think again of the abundance that He so desires to bestow on His obedient children, I am humbled in the presence of such great love.

I know that like me you long to experience the fullness of His love. Otherwise you wouldn't have put in the time and effort to follow me on this journey to learn about the Father's desire to bring prosperity into our lives.

Yet perhaps you may be struggling deep inside. As much as you want to obey the Lord in the area of biblical giving, you just can't see how it's possible. Or you know, as I do, that with God *nothing* is impossible, but you don't know where to begin. God has called me to preach His glorious Word, and in this chapter I want to do something that's just a little bit different for me, and that is to give you very concrete suggestions about how you can start on the biblical road to blessing. It is an old saying but a true one that a journey of a thousand miles begins with the first step.

In this chapter I'm going to give you a road map that will show you how to experience the biblical road to blessing. I'm going to share some practical hints on how to get out of debt, stay out of debt, and manage your money wisely. In a nutshell, here is how to get on the biblical road to blessing:

- Remember you're not alone—God will help you succeed.
- Surrender to God's love—you will see His results when you live His way.
- Give to God first—remembering His goodness.
- Work hard—remembering you work for Him.
- Provide for your own family members—remembering that God has given them to you.
- Make a budget—remembering the Lord will give you power over satan's strategies.
- Provide for others—remembering the best investment is for eternity.

Remember You're Not Alone—God Will Help You Succeed

Managing our money is never easy, which is why I'm so thankful that I don't have to rely on my own strength, insight, and willpower in the area of finances. Regardless of my past track record, God's Word is *still* the same: "I can do all things *through Christ* who strengthens me." (Phil. 4:13) That's right, today, *right now*, the power of the Savior is available to us when we make the courageous choice to do His will.

Now when I say this, I don't mean that doing His will in the area of finances will be easy. Indeed, you may even find yourself in a circumstance that appears in the natural to be *absolutely impossible*. This is exactly the situation the Lord *delights* in. That is why I love to sing in the crusades:

> *Nothing is impossible when you put your trust in God*
> *Nothing is impossible when you're trusting in His Word.*
>
> *Hearken to the voice of God to thee,*
> *Is there anything too hard for me?*

Then put your trust, in God alone
And rest upon His Word.
For everything,
Yes everything,
Yes everything is possible with God![1]

God's blessing isn't limited to the steps I'm going to outline below. Rather, these godly disciplines form the core that the Father will surround, energize, and bless. You may need nothing short of a financial miracle, but what is available to you right now is nothing short of a financial miracle. In partnership with the Master, you cannot fail!

Surrender to God's Love—You'll See His Results When You Live His Way

My friend, there is a reason why this chapter comes near the end of this book: the biblical road to blessing is a *relationship*, not a technique. It's not so much a way of *living* as it is a way of *loving*. And the highest form of loving the Father is *surrender*, and surrender manifests itself in *obedience*.

The Lord Jesus cautions us in Luke 12:15, "Take heed and beware of covetousness, for one's life does not consist in the abundance of the things he possesses." Yet you and I are bombarded by messages that our lives *do* consist in the abundance of things, and that we will be happier with just a little more. In fact, in America on an average day, we are exposed to twenty nine new products, eighteen hundred commercial messages per person, and $700 million spent on advertising.[2] It's no wonder that someone has quipped, "If we had our lives to live over again . . . we'd need more money!"

Because of all these factors, the words of Jesus aren't merely a parable on the human condition, they are a commentary on the current state: "Still others, like seed sown among thorns, hear the word; but the worries of this life, the deceitfulness of wealth and the desires for other things come in and choke the word, making it unfruitful." (Mark 4:18–19 NIV)

I declare to you in the name of the Lord that you can be completely and permanently set free in a moment if you will let the Holy Spirit have His way. You can stop right now and bow before the Lord and find freedom from financial bondage by surrender to His wonderful will.

Give to God First— Remembering His Goodness

The fastest way to breakthrough with your finances is to pay God first. The principle of firstfruits is dynamic and timeless:

> "Honor the LORD with your possessions,
> And with the firstfruits of all your increase;
> So your barns will be filled with plenty,
> And your vats will overflow with new wine.
> (Prov. 3:9–10)

I know that like me, you take very seriously all of your responsibilities, and that includes your financial obligations. Perhaps your mind is racing ahead of me, thinking, *But, Pastor Benny, I owe $5,000 to MasterCard, and I only have $30 left over after paying for just the essentials like housing, food, and basic transportation. How can I pay a tithe before I pay my other bills and still be responsible?*

My answer is as simple as it is liberating: the most responsible thing you can do is pay God first. You see, the Father wants so much for you to experience abundance, but you miss His abundance if you do not express your love through obedience. As we have discussed at length in earlier chapters, He wants you to give to Him first and to give to Him your best. When you pay God's bills, you'll be amazed to see how He'll pay *your* bills.

If you earn $2,500 a month, *the absolute first thing* you

need to do after you are paid is to write out a check for $250 as your tithe. Give that money to the place where you are fed spiritually. For most Christians that is the local church they attend. Even though you may have huge debts and you despair that you will ever break even, always give your tithe first—and do it not grudgingly, but with expectation. I can tell you from experience and without fear of refutation that God will bless the 90 percent you have left in ways that will make it go much farther than 100 percent can ever go without His blessing.

One thing He will do is make you wiser with your money. Now that you are honoring Him with your first-fruits, some of the things you used to spend your money on may no longer entice you. When you delight yourself in the Lord, He gives you the desires of your heart. And at least part of what this verse means is that He ennobles your desires. Suddenly, you find that you are experiencing His great abundance. And because there is now "no lack," God will meet your needs and help you pay off your debts. Remember, you don't tithe *in order* for your bills to be paid; rather, you tithe in love *in expectation* that the Father desires more than anything to bless you abundantly, and is standing by "to do exceedingly abundantly above all that [you] ask or think, according to the power that works in [you]." (Eph. 3:20)

Work Hard—Remembering You Work for Him

Because of the sacrifice on the cross of the precious Lord Jesus, all who believe in Him are adopted into His family as sons. With sonship comes the many wonderful blessings that we've looked at together in this book. But never forget that membership in any family carries with it not only benefits but responsibilities as well. And as believers, we have a responsibility to work *hard*, for the Scriptures declare in Colossians 3:22–24: "Bondservants, obey in all things your masters according to the flesh, not with eyeservice, as men-pleasers, but in sincerity of heart, fearing God. And whatever you do, do it heartily, as to the Lord and not to men, knowing that from the Lord you will receive the reward of the inheritance; for you serve the Lord Christ.''

That's the secret: we don't work for our employers as we work for the Lord. And although payday of one sort occurs every week or two weeks or month, never forget that there is another, better "paycheck" being prepared for you by the Lord.

God is not a genie who exists to grant us wishes. We have to do more to enjoy the Father's blessing than merely rub a lamp. But when we do work hard, the Lord unequivocally rewards us with blessing, for the Word of God says:

> The soul of a lazy man desires, and has nothing;
> But the soul of the diligent shall be made rich. (Prov. 13:4)

> Do you see a man who excels in his work?
> He will stand before kings;
> He will not stand before unknown men. (Prov. 22:29)

Provide for Your Own Family Members— Remembering that God Has Given Them to You

Next to the salvation we enjoy through faith in the Lord Jesus, the most precious gift God has given us is our families. And with this privilege comes the sacred responsibility that we do all in our power to provide for them. For the apostle Paul solemnly specified in 1 Timothy 5:8, ''But if anyone does not provide for his own, and especially for those of his household, he has denied the faith and is worse than an unbeliever.''

Under God, your family is your responsibility. If you have child support payments to make, make them. If you're out of work, find work. If you need to be retrained, seek retraining. If you need to move to be where the jobs are, then move.

But remember, your family is your responsibility, and as you take seriously your obligation to provide for them, as I know you do, the Lord *will* make a way for you to do just that. I know how hard this can be sometimes in our changing economy, but I also know that David's declaration in the Word of God is as true today as it was then, "I have been young, and now am old; Yet I have not seen the righteous forsaken, Nor his descendants begging bread." (Ps. 37:25)

Make a budget— Remembering the Lord Will Give You Power over Satan's Strategies

The Blessing of a Budget

Once we begin to understand the great love of our heavenly Father for His children and surrender ourselves completely and without reserve to that love, we begin to have confidence and boldness. Yet our Father wants us to live not only in *boldness*, but in *wisdom* as well. Boldness manifests itself in surrender to God, and wisdom manifests itself in the setting of a *budget*. In Proverbs 21:5, King Solomon declared:

"*The plans* of the diligent lead surely to plenty,
But those of everyone who is hasty, surely to poverty.

You see, budgeting is simply *forming and following a plan for plenty*.

In its most simple form, a budget is a way of tracking what is coming in and where it is going. When you have a clear idea of these two things, you can know your present position and then plan for the future. All of your budget decisions are just as spiritual as the decision to honor the

Lord with your tithes and offerings. Ron Blue was so penetrating when he observed:

> [An] implication of believing that God owns it all is that
> every spending decision is, in reality, a spiritual deci-
> sion. There is nothing more or less spiritual about giv-
> ing a tithe than spending money on a vacation. If, in
> fact, it is all God's money to begin with, then implicitly
> whenever I make a spending decision, I am saying that
> this is what God would have done with His resources.
> This should free us to use God's resources for the ac-
> complishment of the goals and desires that God places
> in our hearts, with no feelings of guilt. This, of course,
> implies that one is also listening to God on a regular
> basis to determine what He would have done with His
> resources.[3]

Find Out Where Your Money Is Going Out

I won't go into all of the specifics of setting up a budget
here because there are many good materials on this topic, a
number of which I have listed for you in the back of the
book. However, I do want to underline for you the importance of a realistic budget in getting and staying on the
biblical road to blessing. Begin by determining where the
money is going—that is, your expenses.

Most people break their expenses into two groups—
fixed and unfixed. Fixed expenses are ones that are the
same every month and include expenses such as your rent
or mortgage, taxes, utilities, debt payments, and so on. *You
should include your tithe in this group.* Unfixed expenses are
ones that vary from month to month and include expenses
such as food, clothing, entertainment, and vacations. No
matter how you do it, you must find out just how much
money is going out and where—each month.

Find Out How Much Money Is Coming In

Once you have your expenses listed, then you need to list all of your income. The difference between your income and your expenses lets you know the general state of your finances. If you make but a penny *more* than you spend, you can be on the road to finding peace. If you make but a penny *less* than you spend, peace will forever elude you.

Most people who engage in this exercise are amazed to discover that they are spending more than they are making, or if there is any excess, it is very small. Your goal with your budget will be to get to a point—after your debts are taken care of—where you have money left over.

If you find your "outgoing" is more than your "incoming," don't feel alone or be discouraged. After all, the Lord *wants* to prosper you, and you are making the wonderful decision to obey Him! Even though you have some work to do, this can be a *tremendously* exciting time because of the information you have now gathered.

Search Your Expenses for Savings

Here are some steps to take. First, in an atmosphere of prayer, dependence, and faith in God, go through your unfixed expenses and lift them up before the Lord. Ask yourself on each item, Is there a smarter or less expensive way to do this? In this section of your budget the Master will give you insight and allow you to see some exciting possibilities about how you can spend your money more effectively. Your first goal is to get out of debt and then to make sure that your spending is under control. That could mean that you will have some uncomfortable choices to make because most new things seem a little uncomfortable and awkward initially. But, oh, my friend, the result will be freedom and joy that you may have never known!

Let me give you an example of a way you might discover to spend your money with more wisdom. If you make your own lunch instead of buying one, you might save $2 or so every working day. That doesn't sound like very much, but in the course of a month that can add up to more than $40! If you're able to identify just two more areas like this, you'll have discovered more than $120 a month that you can use to move toward freedom from debt—after you've paid the Lord His tithes, that is. And think of how much farther this money will go with God's hand of blessing upon it!

Most likely, when you finish prayerfully evaluating your budget in the area of unfixed expenses, you will have made some exciting gains. You might not even need to look at your fixed expenses. Think of what a blessing that would be!

But if you still are just breaking even or have only a small positive cash flow, there is much more that can still be done, for you can move forward and look at your fixed costs. Sometimes the options appear more limited, but the Master *will* give you a breakthrough.

Consider these examples. What about your rent or home mortgage? Is it possible you are living in a more expensive home than you can afford? Should you consider moving to a less-expensive rental or selling your home and finding one that better fits your means? What about your car situation? Are you locked into a high payment when you could get by with a car that isn't quite so expensive? Remember, "little is much when God is with it." As you get on the biblical road to blessing by obedience, you may very well find that you live in a nicer house or drive a nicer car for which you have paid less money. Or you may find that the contentment that the Lord gives you is so rich that you care very little about where you live and what car you drive, for you are caught up in the wonderful love of the Father.

And don't forget that you don't have to go through this process alone. Not only will the presence of God surround you, but He has also given financial insight to people in your own congregation and through fine Christian books and tapes. Seek out and rely on wise counsel for the Scripture declares, "In the multitude of counselors there is safety." (Prov. 11:14)

Determine to Be Debt-Free . . .

God does not want His children living in the bondage of debt. I'm absolutely convinced of this truth.

Sometimes we need to consider taking on a reasonable and limited amount of debt, perhaps to buy a home. But perhaps the best thing you can ever do related to managing your finances is to make the decision to never go into debt—at least not for things that don't grow in value over time. How many people do you know, for instance, who owe more on their automobile than it is worth? What bondage! And bondage that the Master never intended for us to experience.

In the U.S., though, where it's so easy to get credit and the advertisers tempt us non-stop to buy more and more, all too many people end up in debt. And although we're bombarded with temptation every day, it is still as true as ever that "He who is in you is greater than he who is in the world." (John 4:4) So let me give you a few practical ideas about getting out of debt.

Most advisors on finances say it's best to concentrate on just one debt at a time. Often a good way to start is to tackle the one with the lowest balance. If you have many debts, you will need to keep making the minimum payment on all of them.

Debt	Balance Owed	Minimum Payment	What You Actually Pay	
Sears	$1,000	$40	$40 + the extra you find in the budget + the extra God gives you	Concentrate on this first
Visa	$2,000	$80	$80	
Mastercard	$3,000	$120	$120	
Total	$6,000	$240	$240 +	

Once the Lord has provided and you are completely free of the first debt, concentrate completely on the second debt, allocating *at least* as much money to your debts as before.

Debt	Balance Owed	Minimum Payment	What You Actually Pay	
Visa	$2,000	$80	$80 + $40 + the extra you find in the budget + the extra God gives you	Now concentrate here
Mastercard	$3,000	$120	$120	
Total	$5,000	$200	$240 +	

Amount Paid per Month
Stays the Same

Then keep doing this until all of your debts are completely paid. Be sure to keep a list of your debts handy. What joy you'll know as one by one you are able to praise God for a debt paid and another step on the road to financial freedom!

. . . And Keep Being Determined

Sticking with a budget requires diligence. I don't know why, but it's so easy to conveniently "forget" and buy "just this little thing." But remember, you don't have to give in, for as the apostle Paul declared in 2 Timothy 1:7, "God did not give us a spirit of timidity, but a spirit of power, of love and of self-discipline."

You'll find that one of the most effective tools at your disposal to stay on your budget is a notebook to keep track of where the money is going. You don't need a computer and a college degree in math to do this. The key is that you must stay at it by getting receipts and writing down what you are spending and then checking on how you are doing— never forgetting that as you are doing this, the Lord is in the process of blessing you beyond all that you can ask or even imagine." (Eph. 3:20)

If you are married, you will enjoy the special blessing that comes when you make a commitment to experience the blessing of a budget *as a team.* In fact, if you include your children in this process, you will not only see greater unity in your family, but also have the satisfaction of knowing that you are passing on sound financial advice to the next generation.

I encourage you to use a three-by-five-inch card and write down not only your financial goals, but also the basic principles on prosperity in the Word of God that the Holy Spirit has strongly impressed upon your heart. Such principles might include ideas like these:

- The heavenly Father's desire to bless
- The joy of obedience
- Giving not to receive a harvest, but in expectation of the harvest
- Becoming debt-free

Take these goals and principles with you wherever you go. When you are considering whether to buy an item, your decision might become clearer if you remind yourself of your goals. This constant reminder of your goals will help you keep your personal budget in perspective.

Set Up a Storehouse

The storehouse is God's idea. In listing the blessings of obedience in Deuteronomy 28, the Word declares, "The LORD will command the blessing on you in your storehouses and in all to which you set your hand, and He will bless you in the land which the Lord your God is giving you." (v. 8) Another term for storehouse is *savings account.*[4]

In Old Testament times, storehouses were set up to make sure that enough provisions, such as grain for food, would be available if a famine or some other disaster occurred. Joseph was one of the first to do this when he made the Egyptians save grain for seven years. When the seven years of famine came, plenty of food was available, indeed enough to feed members of Joseph's own family. (Gen. 41–48)

The point is that it's not just a good idea—it's God's idea—to set aside some of your earnings in savings. God is not saying you should hoard money, but it is prudent to have some extra resources set aside for your unexpected needs or the unexpected needs of others. How wonderful it is to hear about a need and when prompted by the Holy Spirit to have the resources to help meet the need—without going into debt!

The apostle Paul alluded to this practice when he advised the Corinthians, "Now concerning the collection for the saints, as I have given orders to the churches of Galatia, so you must do also: On the first day of the week let each one of you lay something aside, storing up as he may prosper, that there be no collections when I come. And when I come, whomever you approve by your letters I will send to bear your gift to Jerusalem." (1 Cor. 16:1–3) Notice that they were to lay aside money on Sunday for their personal storehouse so that when Paul or his emissaries visited, the offering would be ready and waiting. Even if you're in debt, it's a good idea to budget a small amount for your personal storehouse.

When you are out of debt, how much should you try to save? I believe that the Word of God gives you latitude in this area. You should use your God-given common sense. If you are in an occupation that is seasonal and you may face long periods without work, then you need to save more than someone who has a very stable income. A good round number to start with is 10 percent, meaning you would tithe 10 percent to the Lord and then aim to save 10 percent and live on the other 80 percent. But part of this adventure will be letting the Holy Spirit guide you.

The important issue is that we maintain a balance between having too little and too much. By this I mean that we have enough in our storehouse to take care of emergencies and special opportunities to give, but not too much so that we begin to depend on our money as our source of security. But never forget that we trust in the *Lord*, not in our *finances*.

The parable that our blessed Master told of the man who trusted in his riches is as appropriate today as ever. In this passage we read,

And He said to them, "Take heed and beware of covetousness, for one's life does not consist in the abundance of the things he possesses." Then He spoke a parable to them, saying: "The ground of a certain rich man yielded plentifully. And he thought within himself, saying, 'What shall I do, since I have no room to store my crops?' So he said, 'I will do this: I will pull down my barns and build greater, and there I will store all my crops and my goods. And I will say to my soul, "Soul, you have many goods laid up for many years; take your ease; eat, drink, and be merry.'' ' But God said to him, 'Fool! This night your soul will be required of you; then whose will those things be which you have provided?' So is he who lays up treasure for himself, and is not rich toward God.'' (Luke 12:15–21)

Be Aware of Satan's Strategies

The Lord Jesus plainly declared in John 10:10, ''The thief does not come except to steal, and to kill, and to destroy. I have come that they may have life, and that they may have it more abundantly.'' The techniques that satan uses to steal, kill, and destroy are ones that he has used repeatedly and refined skillfully. But his techniques are not secret, nor are we ignorant of them, for the apostle Paul declared in 2 Corinthians 2:11 (NASB), ''In order that no advantage be taken of us by satan; for we are not ignorant of his schemes.''

One of satan's particularly destructive areas to practice his schemes is in the area of finances. Indeed, the experts in personal finance agree that certain situations are a problem for many people. I call them money traps, and we are wise to know what they are and to stay far away. Yet as problematic as these things are, you and I *can be and are* more than conquerors through Him who loved us and gave Himself for us. Here are nine of satan's favorite financial schemes.

1. Entice you to buy with credit cards:

These little pieces of plastic can become the monsters of debt! Almost everyone who has a serious problem with debt has misused credit cards. It isn't just the major cards such as Visa or MasterCard that can become a problem. Almost every store you walk into wants to put more plastic in your billfold. But you don't need more credit cards or higher credit limits. You need the blessing of the Father, which is available through obedience. When you have been preapproved by the Father, you don't need to be preapproved by anyone else. Yet in almost every situation, buying with a credit card can put you in danger and distract you from your financial goals.

Of course, sometimes you may need a credit card to make an emergency or extraordinary purchase. If that happens, make it your goal to set aside money to pay off the whole amount immediately—in fact, try to write out a check to the credit card company the same day.

Most of the time, though, I recommend that you only have one or two credit cards *and leave them in a safe place at home.* If you don't carry them with you, you will be that much less tempted to make poor buying decisions. Doing this will afford you a much-needed cooling-off period as you return home to get your credit card to think about whether you really feel strongly about a purchase—and are willing to incur the debt necessary to buy it.

2. Entice you to consider only the "Minimum monthly payment" or "low monthly payment":

This trap is related to credit cards. If you run up some debt on your card, the monthly statement will require you to make only a small minimum monthly payment. This sounds so nice—anyone can pay $10 or $20 on the card, then go buy more! That's what the credit card people want you to do—buy more. And in the meantime you will pay a high rate of interest every month. And if you don't stop buying with the card, that minimum payment may never get your bill paid off because the interest will grow almost as fast as your payment.

Also, think about how many times you have been looking at a car or thinking of buying a major appliance and the salesperson promised with the most engaging smile, "You can own this for only $99 a month. You can afford only $99 a month, can't you?" And many of us conclude that we can afford just $99 a month. The problem is that the salesperson may not mention that the interest rate is so high that you'll be paying "only $99 a month" for sixty months! Always find out the total cost of what you are buying—including interest. Then you can decide if "just $99 a month" is such a great deal after all.

3. Entice you to buy impulsively from mail order catalogs:

Virtually every day one of those glossy, four-color catalogs shows up in the mailbox. It's so convenient. All you need to do is call an 800 number (a "free" call) and use—guess what!—your credit card. This may be the easiest way of all to go in debt. If catalogs are too tempting to you, have your name taken off the mailing list. Or put the catalog in the garbage can on your way to the house from the mailbox.

4. Entice you to shop for groceries when you're hungry:

Most financial experts give this advice. The more hungry you are, the more likely you will fill your cart with what looks good at the moment. If your stomach is full when you go shopping, it will be easier to concentrate on your shopping list—not how hungry you are.

5. Entice you to waste money and time on get-rich-quick schemes:

Someone once said that if "something is too good to be true, *it is* too good to be true!" Late-night infomercials would have you believe that riches are just an 800 call away. If they really were, wouldn't everyone be rich? Don't fall for get-rich-quick schemes, regardless of the source. If you have questions about some money-making opportunity, ask questions until you have good answers. And don't hesitate to get advice from others.

6. Entice you to waste money and time on gambling:

Hopefully, this is obvious to you, but with so much gambling throughout the United States, more and more people are thinking it might be a way to get rich or get out of debt. Nothing could be farther from the truth! Don't waste your money. Instead of playing those scratch games or Lotto, put the money that the Father has entrusted to you into paying off your debt or into your storehouse to provide for yourself and bless others. Then instead of throwing away your money, you'll delight the Father by investing for eternity.

7. Entice you to spend too much on holiday and gift spending:

It's a sad truth that many Christians start getting into financial trouble because they buy too many Christmas presents on credit. I'll bet satan gets a big laugh from exploiting our celebrations of the birth of our dear Savior to bring us into unholy and joy-stealing financial bondage. Make no mistake. It is a wonderful thing to give gifts to others, just as our heavenly Father gives gifts to us. But we need to use common sense, stick to our financial goals and budget, and pay cash! It is trite but *so* true that it is the thoughtfulness of the gift and not its cost that is ultimately important—and meaningful.

8. Entice you to make financial decisions without your spouse:

If you are married, your spouse needs to be your partner in making money decisions. Both of you should agree on the family's financial goals and understand the budget. Talk to each other and pray together about how to use the Lord's money. Money squabbles cause more hurt in marriages than virtually any other issue, and often the disagreements become so serious that divorce results. Don't let this happen in your home. Be a team concerning your finances.

9. Entice you to buy things that are of no real usefulness to you:

How many things do you have sitting in the garage or a

ऀऀऀऀऀऀ

ऀऀऀ

closet that you have hardly ever used and now don't know what to do with? Did you really need that gadget in the first place? And don't get me wrong. I'm not saying that every purchase has to be a *necessity* in order to be Biblical. After all, our God delights to give us good things. But nevertheless you are exercising godly wisdom if you are very careful about buying things that don't have some useful purpose in your day-to-day life—and selling or giving away those things that are doing nothing for you other than taking up space.

10. Entice you into cosigning a loan for someone else:
Many good relationships with family members and friends have been ruined by signing a loan on someone else's behalf. There may be a wonderful reason to co-sign a loan, but never forget that in so doing *you* assume the responsibility when the loan comes due—and you may very well end up paying it or having *your* credit damaged in the process. If you are prayerfully willing to take the risk and have the resources to pay such a loan, then you may certainly want to help someone out in this way. Just be sure to carefully study Proverbs 6:1–5 first.
I could say much more, but these are the most deadly strategies of the evil one. Many good books and tapes are available. Ask for recommendations at your church, or stop by a Christian bookstore to find the materials you need.

Provide for Others— Remembering the Best Investment Is for Eternity.

The apostle Paul gave us this all-inclusive mandate to those who are of the household of faith in Galatians 6:10, when he declares, "Therefore as we have opportunity, let us do good to all, especially to those who are of the household of faith." Now let's examine this marvelous verse phrase by phrase:
• "As we have opportunity"—after we have been obedient in the area of tithing and providing adequately for ourselves

and our families. You see, we don't really have the *opportunity* to provide for others if we have yet to be obedient in the area of tithing and providing for ourselves and our families.

- "Let us do good to all"—people outside our families whom we can bless.
- "Especially to those who are of the household of faith"—provide financially *first* to those who bear the name of the Lord, *then* to those who do not.

When we follow this simple, practical, and biblical strategy, not only are we embarking upon the biblical road to blessing, but we will discover the secret that Norman Macewan alluded to when he declared:

> Happiness is not so much
> in having or sharing.
> We make a living
> by what we get,
> but we make a life
> by what we give.[5]

Exceedingly Great and Precious Promises

Promises to Partake . . . and Escape

Oh, how I love the encouragement the apostle Peter set before us when he declared in 2 Peter 1:3–11:

His divine power has given to us all things that pertain to life and godliness, through the knowledge of Him who called us by glory and virtue, by which have been given to us exceedingly great and precious promises, that through these you may be partakers of the divine nature, having escaped the corruption that is in the world through lust. But also for this very reason, giving all diligence, add to your faith virtue, to virtue knowledge, to knowledge self-control, to self-control perseverance, to perseverance godliness, to godliness brotherly kindness, and to brotherly kindness love. For if these things are yours and abound, you will be neither barren nor unfruitful in the knowledge of our Lord Jesus Christ. For he who lacks these things is shortsighted, even to blindness, and has forgotten that he was cleansed from his old sins. Therefore, brethren, be even more diligent to make your call and election sure, for if

you do these things you will never stumble; for so an
entrance will be supplied to you abundantly into the
everlasting kingdom of our Lord and Savior Jesus
Christ.

Every single thing that results in *life* and *godliness* is found
in the Lord Jesus. The apostle Peter in this mountaintop
passage of Scripture called special attention to the promises
the Master gave us in His Word. As we live the truth of the
promises of the Word, the Father delights to hold out for us
not only that we can partake of the divine nature, but also
that we can "escape the corruption in the world caused by
evil desires." (2 Peter 1:4 NIV) Truly, we *are* "more than
conquerors through Him who loved us." (Rom. 8:37)

Promises . . . That Will Come True

The report of King Solomon to the assembly of
Israel is just as true today as it was when he delivered it so long ago, declaring in 1 Kings 8:56,
"Blessed be the LORD, who has given rest to His
people Israel, according to all that He promised. There has not failed one word of all His
good promise, which He promised through His
servant Moses." I began this book with a song,
and I want to remind you again of a portion of its lyrics:

For with God, nothing is impossible!
It's not possible to be impossible.
And with God, every promise shall come true,
For we know surely all things He can do.[1]

Promises . . . For the Faithful Giver

In this portion of the book, I have selected 129 key promises from the Word of God that I believe will give you the challenge and encouragement you need to surrender to the will of God and watch with expectation and confidence for Him to bless you. Never forget that we surrender in obedience *not in order to* be blessed, but *in expectation of* blessing because we know of the Father's great love and generosity for His children.

Here is what I suggest you do to get the maximum benefit both out of this chapter and out of the book. Incorporate these promises and passages into your daily time of prayer and Bible study. If you read one or two portions in the morning and another portion or two in the evening, you will read through these promises in a month or two. If you concentrate on just one portion a day, you will go through them in about four months. Be sure to underline them, highlight them, and make notes as you study the promises. Find them in your Bible and study the context. Also, don't forget to read them *repeatedly*. After you've gone through them, go through them again and again! The Holy Spirit will particularly impress certain ones on your heart. Consider writing those passages down on a three-by-five card and carrying them with you in your purse or wallet.

1. Genesis 1:26–28

Then God said, "Let Us make man in Our image, according to Our likeness; let them have dominion over the fish of the sea, over the birds of the air, and over the cattle, over all the earth and over every creeping thing that creeps on the earth." So God created man in His own image; in the image of God He created him; male and female He created them. Then God blessed them, and God said to them, "Be fruitful and multiply; fill the earth and subdue it; have dominion over the fish of the sea, over the birds of the air, and over every living thing that moves on the earth."

2. Genesis 22:15–17

Then the Angel of the LORD called to Abraham a second
time out of heaven, and said: "By Myself I have sworn, says
the LORD, because you have done this thing, and have not
withheld your son, your only son—blessing I will bless you,
and multiplying I will multiply your descendants as the stars
of the heaven and as the sand which is on the seashore; and
your descendants shall possess the gate of their enemies."

3. Exodus 12:36

And the LORD had given the people favor in the sight of the
Egyptians, so that they granted them what they requested.
Thus they plundered the Egyptians.

4. Leviticus 26:3–9

If you walk in My statutes and keep My commandments, and
perform them, then I will give you rain in its season, the
land shall yield its produce, and the trees of the field shall
yield their fruit. Your threshing shall last till the time of
vintage, and the vintage shall last till the time of sowing; you
shall eat your bread to the full, and dwell in your land safely.
I will give peace in the land, and you shall lie down, and
none will make you afraid; I will rid the land of evil beasts,
and the sword will not go through your land. You will chase
your enemies, and they shall fall by the sword before you.
Five of you shall chase a hundred, and a hundred of you
shall put ten thousand to flight; your enemies shall fall by
the sword before you. For I will look on you favorably and
make you fruitful, multiply you and confirm My covenant
with you.

5. Numbers 6:22–27

And the LORD spoke to Moses, saying: "Speak to Aaron and
his sons, saying, 'This is the way you shall bless the children
of Israel. Say to them:
"The LORD bless you and keep you;

The LORD make His face shine upon you,
And be gracious to you;
The *LORD lift up His countenance upon you,
And give you peace." '*
So they shall put My name on the children of Israel, and I
will bless them."

6. *Deuteronomy 8:18*

And you shall remember the LORD your God, for it is He
who gives you power to get wealth, that He may establish
His covenant which He swore to your fathers, as it is this
day.

7. *Deuteronomy 14:22–23*

You shall truly tithe all the increase of your grain that the
field produces year by year. And you shall eat before the
LORD your God, in the place where He chooses to make His
name abide, the tithe of your grain and your new wine and
your oil, of the firstborn of your herds and your flocks, that
you may learn to fear the LORD your God always.

8. *Deuteronomy 26:1–2, 18–19*

And it shall be, when you come into the land which the
LORD your God is giving you as an inheritance, and you possess it and dwell in it, that you shall take some of the first of
all the produce of the ground, which you shall bring from
your land that the LORD your God is giving you, and put it in
a basket and go to the place where the LORD your God
chooses to make His name abide. . . . Also today the LORD
has proclaimed you to be His special people, just as He
promised you, that you should keep all His commandments,
and that He will set you high above all nations which He has
made, in praise, in name, and in honor, and that you may
be a holy people to the LORD your God, just as He has spoken.

9. Deuteronomy 28:1–13

Now it shall come to pass, if you diligently obey the voice of the LORD your God, to observe carefully all His commandments which I command you today, that the LORD your God will set you high above all nations of the earth. And all these blessings shall come upon you and overtake you, because you obey the voice of the LORD your God: Blessed shall you be in the city, and blessed shall you be in the country. Blessed shall be the fruit of your body, the produce of your ground and the increase of your herds, the increase of your cattle and the offspring of your flocks. Blessed shall be your basket and your kneading bowl. Blessed shall you be when you come in, and blessed shall you be when you go out. The LORD will cause your enemies who rise against you to be defeated before your face; they shall come out against you one way and flee before you seven ways. The LORD will command the blessing on you in your storehouses and in all to which you set your hand, and He will bless you in the land which the LORD your God is giving you. The LORD will establish you as a holy people to Himself, just as He has sworn to you, if you keep the commandments of the LORD your God and walk in His ways. Then all peoples of the earth shall see that you are called by the name of the LORD, and they shall be afraid of you. And the LORD will grant you plenty of goods, in the fruit of your body, in the increase of your livestock, and in the produce of your ground, in the land of which the LORD swore to your fathers to give you. The LORD will open to you His good treasure, the heavens, to give the rain to your land in its season, and to bless all the work of your hand. You shall lend to many nations, but you shall not borrow. And the LORD will make you the head and not the tail; you shall be above only, and not be beneath, if you heed the commandments of the LORD your God, which I command you today, and are careful to observe them.

10. *Deuteronomy 33:27*

> The eternal God is your refuge,
> And underneath are the everlasting arms;
> He will thrust out the enemy from before you,
> And will say, "Destroy!"

11. *Joshua 1:8*

> This Book of the Law shall not depart from your mouth, but you shall meditate in it day and night, that you may observe to do according to all that is written in it. For then you will make your way prosperous, and then you will have good success.

12. *Judges 5:12–13*

> Awake, awake, Deborah!
> Awake, awake, sing a song!
> Arise, Barak, and lead your captives away,
> O son of Abinoam!
> Then the survivors came down, the people against the nobles;
> The LORD came down for me against the mighty.

13. *Ruth 4:15*

> And may he be to you a restorer of life and a nourisher of your old age; for your daughter-in-law, who loves you, who is better to you than seven sons, has borne him.

14. *First Samuel 2:27–30*

> Then a man of God came to Eli and said to him, "Thus says the LORD: 'Did I not clearly reveal Myself to the house of your father when they were in Egypt in Pharaoh's house? Did I not choose him out of all the tribes of Israel to be My priest, to offer upon My altar, to burn incense, and to wear an ephod before Me? And did I not give to the house of your father all the offerings of the children of Israel made by fire? Why do you kick at My sacrifice and My offering

which I have commanded in My dwelling place, and honor your sons more than Me, to make yourselves fat with the best of all the offerings of Israel My people?' Therefore the LORD God of Israel says: 'I said indeed that your house and the house of your father would walk before Me forever.' But now the LORD says: 'Far be it from Me; for *those who honor Me I will honor,* and those who despise Me shall be lightly esteemed.' "

15. Second Samuel 22:17–20, 29–37

He sent from above, He took me,
He drew me out of many waters.
He delivered me from my strong enemy,
From those who hated me;
For they were too strong for me.
They confronted me in the day of my calamity,
But the LORD was my support.
He also brought me out into a broad place;
He delivered me because He delighted in me. . . .
For You are my lamp, O LORD;
The LORD shall enlighten my darkness.
For by You I can run against a troop;
By my God I can leap over a wall.
As for God, His way is perfect;
The word of the LORD is proven;
He is a shield to all who trust in Him.
For who is God, except the LORD?
And who is a rock, except our God?
God is my strength and power,
And He makes my way perfect.
He makes my feet like the feet of deer,
And sets me on my high places.
He teaches my hands to make war,
So that my arms can bend a bow of bronze.
You have also given me the shield of Your salvation;
Your gentleness has made me great.

You enlarged my path under me;
So my feet did not slip.

16. *First Kings 2:1-3*

Now the days of David drew near that he should die, and he charged Solomon his son, saying: "I go the way of all the earth; be strong, therefore, and prove yourself a man. And keep the charge of the LORD your God: to walk in His ways, to keep His statutes, His commandments, His judgments, and His testimonies, as it is written in the Law of Moses, that you may prosper in all that you do and wherever you turn."

17. *First Kings 8:56*

Blessed be the LORD, who has given rest to His people Israel, according to all that He promised. There has not failed one word of all His good promise, which He promised through His servant Moses.

18. *First Kings 17:10-16*

So he arose and went to Zarephath. And when he came to the gate of the city, indeed a widow was there gathering sticks. And he called to her and said, "Please bring me a little water in a cup, that I may drink." And as she was going to get it, he called to her and said, "Please bring me a morsel of bread in your hand." So she said, "As the LORD your God lives, I do not have bread, only a handful of flour in a bin, and a little oil in a jar; and see, I am gathering a couple of sticks that I may go in and prepare it for myself and my son, that we may eat it, and die." And Elijah said to her, "Do not fear; go and do as you have said, but make me a small cake from it first, and bring it to me; and afterward make some for yourself and your son. For thus says the LORD God of Israel: 'The bin of flour shall not be used up, nor shall the jar of oil run dry, until the day the LORD sends rain on the earth.' " So she went away and did according to the word of Elijah; and she and he and her household ate for

many days. The bin of flour was not used up, nor did the jar
of oil run dry, according to the word of the LORD which He
spoke by Elijah.

19. Second Kings 4:1–7

A certain woman of the wives of the sons of the prophets
cried out to Elisha, saying, "Your servant my husband is
dead, and you know that your servant feared the LORD. And
the creditor is coming to take my two sons to be his slaves."
So Elisha said to her, "What shall I do for you? Tell me,
what do you have in the house?" And she said, "Your maidservant has nothing in the house but a jar of oil." Then he
said, "Go, borrow vessels from everywhere, from all your
neighbors—empty vessels; do not gather just a few. And
when you have come in, you shall shut the door behind you
and your sons; then pour it into all those vessels, and set
aside the full ones." So she went from him and shut the
door behind her and her sons, who brought the vessels to
her; and she poured it out. Now it came to pass, when the
vessels were full, that she said to her son, "Bring me another vessel." And he said to her, "There is not another
vessel." So the oil ceased. Then she came and told the man
of God. And he said, "Go, sell the oil and pay your debt;
and you and your sons live on the rest."

20. First Chronicles 29:10–13

Therefore David blessed the LORD before all the assembly;
and David said:
"Blessed are You, LORD God of Israel, our Father, forever
and ever.
Yours, O LORD, is the greatness,
The power and the glory,
The victory and the majesty;
For all that is in heaven and in earth is Yours;
Yours is the kingdom, O LORD,
And You are exalted as head over all.

Both riches and honor come from You,
And You reign over all.
In Your hand is power and might;
In Your hand it is to make great
And to give strength to all.
Now therefore, our God,
We thank You
And praise Your glorious name.

21. *Second Chronicles 20:22–27*

Now when they began to sing and to praise, the LORD set ambushes against the people of Ammon, Moab, and Mount Seir, who had come against Judah; and they were defeated. For the people of Ammon and Moab stood up against the inhabitants of Mount Seir to utterly kill and destroy them. And when they had made an end of the inhabitants of Seir, they helped to destroy one another. So when Judah came to a place overlooking the wilderness, they looked toward the multitude; and there were their dead bodies, fallen on the earth. No one had escaped. When Jehoshaphat and his people came to take away their spoil, they found among them an abundance of valuables on the dead bodies, and precious jewelry, which they stripped off for themselves, more than they could carry away; and they were three days gathering the spoil because there was so much. And on the fourth day they assembled in the Valley of Berachah, for there they blessed the LORD; therefore the name of that place was called The Valley of Berachah until this day. Then they returned, every man of Judah and Jerusalem, with Jehoshaphat in front of them, to go back to Jerusalem with joy, for the LORD had made them rejoice over their enemies.

22. *Second Chronicles 26:5*

He sought God in the days of Zechariah, who had understanding in the visions of God; and as long as he sought the LORD, God made him prosper.

23. *Ezra 8:22–23*

"The hand of our God is upon all those for good who seek Him, but His power and His wrath are against all those who forsake Him." So we fasted and entreated our God for this, and He answered our prayer.

24. *Nehemiah 5:1–4, 11–12*

And there was a great outcry of the people and their wives against their Jewish brethren. For there were those who said, "We, our sons, and our daughters are many; therefore let us get grain, that we may eat and live." There were also some who said, "We have mortgaged our lands and vineyards and houses, that we might buy grain because of the famine." There were also those who said, "We have borrowed money for the king's tax on our lands and vineyards. . . ." [I said,] "Restore now to them, even this day, their lands, their vineyards, their olive groves, and their houses, also a hundredth of the money and the grain, the new wine and the oil, that you have charged them." So they said, "We will restore it, and will require nothing from them; we will do as you say." Then I called the priests, and required an oath from them that they would do according to this promise.

25. *Esther 2:15*

And Esther obtained favor in the sight of all who saw her.

26. *Job 5:19–22*

He shall deliver you in six troubles,
Yes, in seven no evil shall touch you.
In famine He shall redeem you from death,
And in war from the power of the sword.
You shall be hidden from the scourge of the tongue,
And you shall not be afraid of destruction when it comes.
You shall laugh at destruction and famine,
And you shall not be afraid of the beasts of the earth.

27. Job 8:7

> Though your beginning was small,
> Yet your latter end would increase abundantly.

28. Job 8:20–22

> Behold, God will not cast away the blameless,
> Nor will He uphold the evildoers.
> He will yet fill your mouth with laughing,
> And your lips with rejoicing.
> Those who hate you will be clothed with shame,
> And the dwelling place of the wicked will come to nothing.

29. Job 22:21–28

> Now acquaint yourself with Him, and be at peace;
> Thereby good will come to you.
> Receive, please, instruction from His mouth,
> And lay up His words in your heart.
> If you return to the Almighty, you will be built up;
> You will remove iniquity far from your tents.
> Then you will lay your gold in the dust,
> And the gold of Ophir among the stones of the brooks.
> Yes, the Almighty will be your gold
> And your precious silver;
> For then you will have your delight in the Almighty,
> And lift up your face to God.
> You will make your prayer to Him,
> He will hear you,
> And you will pay your vows.
> You will also declare a thing,
> And it will be established for you;
> So light will shine on your ways.

30. Job 27:13–17

This is the portion of a wicked man with God,
And the heritage of oppressors, received from the Almighty:
If his children are multiplied, it is for the sword;
And his offspring shall not be satisfied with bread.
Those who survive him shall be buried in death,
And their widows shall not weep,
Though he heaps up silver like dust,
And piles up clothing like clay—
He may pile it up, but the just will wear it,
And the innocent will divide the silver.

31. Job 42:10, 12

And the LORD restored Job's losses when he prayed for his friends. Indeed the Lord gave Job twice as much as he had before. . . . Now the Lord blessed the latter days of Job more than his beginning; for he had fourteen thousand sheep, six thousand camels, one thousand yoke of oxen, and one thousand female donkeys.

32. Psalm 1:1–3

Blessed is the man
Who walks not in the counsel of the ungodly,
Nor stands in the path of sinners,
Nor sits in the seat of the scornful;
But his delight is in the law of the LORD,
And in His law he meditates day and night.
He shall be like a tree
Planted by the rivers of water,
That brings forth its fruit in its season,
Whose leaf also shall not wither;
And whatever he does shall prosper.

33. *Psalm 23:1*

> The LORD is my shepherd;
> I shall not want.

34. *Psalm 34:8–10*

> Oh, taste and see that the LORD is good;
> Blessed is the man who trusts in Him!
> Oh, fear the LORD, you His saints!
> There is no want to those who fear Him.
> The young lions lack and suffer hunger;
> But those who seek the LORD shall not lack any good
> thing.

35. *Psalm 35:27–28*

> Let them shout for joy and be glad,
> Who favor my righteous cause;
> And let them say continually,
> "Let the LORD be magnified,
> Who has pleasure in the prosperity of His servant."
> And my tongue shall speak of Your righteousness
> And of Your praise all the day long.

36. *Psalm 37:3–9*

> Trust in the LORD, and do good;
> Dwell in the land, and feed on His faithfulness.
> Delight yourself also in the LORD,
> And He shall give you the desires of your heart.
> Commit your way to the LORD,
> Trust also in Him,
> And He shall bring it to pass.
> He shall bring forth your righteousness as the light,
> And your justice as the noonday.
> Rest in the LORD, and wait patiently for Him;
> Do not fret because of him who prospers in his way,
> Because of the man who brings wicked schemes to pass.
> Cease from anger, and forsake wrath;

Do not fret—it only causes harm.
For evildoers shall be cut off;
But those who wait on the LORD,
They shall inherit the earth.

37. Psalm 41:1–3

Blessed is he who considers the poor;
The LORD will deliver him in time of trouble.
The LORD will preserve him and keep him alive,
And he will be blessed on the earth;
You will not deliver him to the will of his enemies.
The LORD will strengthen him on his bed of illness;
You will sustain him on his sickbed.

38. Psalm 68:11–12, 19

The Lord gave the word;
Great was the company of those who proclaimed it:
"Kings of armies flee, they flee,
And she who remains at home divides the spoil. . . ."
Blessed be the Lord,
Who daily loads us with benefits,
The God of our salvation! Selah

39. Psalm 73:23–26

Nevertheless I am continually with You;
You hold me by my right hand.
You will guide me with Your counsel,
And afterward receive me to glory.
Whom have I in heaven but You?
And there is none upon earth that I desire besides You.
My flesh and my heart fail;
But God is the strength of my heart and my portion forever.

40. Psalm 75:6–7

> For exaltation comes neither from the east
> Nor from the west nor from the south.
> But God is the Judge:
> He puts down one,
> And exalts another.

41. Psalm 84:11–12

> For the LORD God is a sun and shield;
> The LORD will give grace and glory;
> No good thing will He withhold
> From those who walk uprightly.
> O LORD of hosts,
> Blessed is the man who trusts in You!

42. Psalm 91:9–16

> Because you have made the LORD, who is my refuge,
> Even the Most High, your dwelling place,
> No evil shall befall you,
> Nor shall any plague come near your dwelling;
> For He shall give His angels charge over you,
> To keep you in all your ways.
> In their hands they shall bear you up,
> Lest you dash your foot against a stone.
> You shall tread upon the lion and the cobra,
> The young lion and the serpent you shall trample under-
> foot.
> Because he has set his love upon Me, therefore I will de-
> liver him;
> I will set him on high, because he has known My name.
> He shall call upon Me, and I will answer him;
> I will be with him in trouble;
> I will deliver him and honor him.
> With long life I will satisfy him,
> And show him My salvation."

43. Psalm 103:1–5

Bless the LORD, O my soul;
And all that is within me, bless His holy name!
Bless the LORD, O my soul,
And forget not all His benefits:
Who forgives all your iniquities,
Who heals all your diseases,
Who redeems your life from destruction,
Who crowns you with lovingkindness and tender mercies,
Who satisfies your mouth with good things,
So that your youth is renewed like the eagle's.

44. Psalm 105:37

He also brought them out with silver and gold,
And there was none feeble among His tribes.

45. Psalm 112

Praise the LORD!
Blessed is the man who fears the LORD,
Who delights greatly in His commandments.
His descendants will be mighty on earth;
The generation of the upright will be blessed.
Wealth and riches will be in his house,
And his righteousness endures forever.
Unto the upright there arises light in the darkness;
He is gracious, and full of compassion, and righteous.
A good man deals graciously and lends;
He will guide his affairs with discretion.
Surely he will never be shaken;
The righteous will be in everlasting remembrance.
He will not be afraid of evil tidings;
His heart is steadfast, trusting in the LORD.
His heart is established;
He will not be afraid,
Until he sees his desire upon his enemies.
He has dispersed abroad,

He has given to the poor;
His righteousness endures forever;
His horn will be exalted with honor.
The wicked will see it and be grieved;
He will gnash his teeth and melt away;
The desire of the wicked shall perish.

46. Psalm 116:12–14

What shall I render to the LORD
For all His benefits toward me?
I will take up the cup of salvation,
And call upon the name of the LORD.
I will pay my vows to the LORD
Now in the presence of all His people.

47. Psalm 118:8–9, 25–26

It is better to trust in the LORD
Than to put confidence in man.
It is better to trust in the LORD
Than to put confidence in princes. . . .
Save now, I pray, O LORD;
O LORD, I pray, send now prosperity.
Blessed is he who comes in the name of the LORD!
We have blessed you from the house of the LORD.

48. Psalm 119:165

Great peace have those who love Your law,
And nothing causes them to stumble.

49. Psalm 132:13–16

For the LORD has chosen Zion;
He has desired it for His dwelling place:
"This is My resting place forever;
Here I will dwell, for I have desired it.
I will abundantly bless her provision;
I will satisfy her poor with bread.

I will also clothe her priests with salvation,
And her saints shall shout aloud for joy."

50. Psalm 136:23–25

Who remembered us in our lowly state,
For His mercy endures forever;
And rescued us from our enemies,
For His mercy endures forever;
Who gives food to all flesh,
For His mercy endures forever.

51. Psalm 137:7–8

Remember, O Lord, against the, sons of Edom
The day of Jerusalem,
Who said, "Raze it, raze it,
To its very foundation!"
O daughter of Babylon, who are to be destroyed,
Happy the one who repays you as you have served us!

52. Psalm 145:18–19

The Lord is near to all who call upon Him,
To all who call upon Him in truth.
He will fulfill the desire of those who fear Him;
He also will hear their cry and save them.

53. Proverbs 3:1–2, 9–10, 13–17, 27–28

My son, do not forget my law,
But let your heart keep my commands;
For length of days and long life
And peace they will add to you. . . .
Honor the Lord with your possessions,
And with the firstfruits of all your increase;
So your barns will be filled with plenty,
And your vats will overflow with new wine. . . .
Happy is the man who finds wisdom,
And the man who gains understanding;

For her proceeds are better than the profits of silver,
And her gain than fine gold.
She is more precious than rubies,
And all the things you may desire cannot compare with
her.
Length of days is in her right hand,
In her left hand riches and honor.
Her ways are ways of pleasantness,
And all her paths are peace. . . .
Do not withhold good from those to whom it is due,
When it is in the power of your hand to do so.
Do not say to your neighbor,
"Go, and come back,
And tomorrow I will give it,"
When you have it with you.

54. *Proverbs 8:17–21*

I love those who love me,
And those who seek me diligently will find me.
Riches and honor are with me,
Enduring riches and righteousness.
My fruit is better than gold, yes, than fine gold,
And my revenue than choice silver.
I traverse the way of righteousness,
In the midst of the paths of justice,
That I may cause those who love me to inherit wealth,
That I may fill their treasuries.

55. *Proverbs 10:3–4, 22–24*

The LORD will not allow the righteous soul to famish,
But He casts away the desire of the wicked.
He who has a slack hand becomes poor,
But the hand of the diligent makes rich. . . .
The blessing of the LORD makes one rich,
And He adds no sorrow with it.
To do evil is like sport to a fool,

But a man of understanding has wisdom.
The fear of the wicked will come upon him,
And the desire of the righteous will be granted.

56. Proverbs 11:24–28

There is one who scatters, yet increases more;
And there is one who withholds more than is right,
But it leads to poverty.
The generous soul will be made rich,
And he who waters will also be watered himself.
The people will curse him who withholds grain,
But blessing will be on the head of him who sells it.
He who earnestly seeks good finds favor,
But trouble will come to him who seeks evil.
He who trusts in his riches will fall,
But the righteous will flourish like foliage.

57. Proverbs 13:4, 11, 18, 21–25

The soul of a lazy man desires, and has nothing;
But the soul of the diligent shall be made rich. . . .
Wealth gained by dishonesty will be diminished,
But he who gathers by labor will increase. . . .
Poverty and shame will come to him who disdains correction,
But he who regards a rebuke will be honored. . . .
Evil pursues sinners,
But to the righteous, good shall be repaid.
A good man leaves an inheritance to his children's children,
But the wealth of the sinner is stored up for the righteous.
Much food is in the fallow ground of the poor,
And for lack of justice there is waste.
He who spares his rod hates his son,
But he who loves him disciplines him promptly.

The righteous eats to the satisfying of his soul,
But the stomach of the wicked shall be in want.

58. Proverbs 15:6

In the house of the righteous there is much treasure,
But in the revenue of the wicked is trouble.

59. Proverbs 18:20

A man's stomach shall be satisfied from the fruit of his mouth,
From the produce of his lips he shall be filled.

60. Proverbs 19:17)

He who has pity on the poor lends to the LORD,
And He will pay back what he has given.

61. Proverbs 22:1–4, 9, 29

A good name is to be chosen rather than great riches,
Loving favor rather than silver and gold.
The rich and the poor have this in common,
The LORD is the maker of them all.
A prudent man foresees evil and hides himself,
But the simple pass on and are punished.
By humility and the fear of the LORD
Are riches and honor and life. . . .
He who has a generous eye will be blessed,
For he gives of his bread to the poor. . . .
Do you see a man who excels in his work?
He will stand before kings;
He will not stand before unknown men.

62. Proverbs 24:3–4, 30–34

Through wisdom a house is built,
And by understanding it is established;
By knowledge the rooms are filled
With all precious and pleasant riches. . . .

I went by the field of the lazy man,
And by the vineyard of the man devoid of understanding;
And there it was, all overgrown with thorns;
Its surface was covered with nettles;
Its stone wall was broken down.
When I saw it, I considered it well;
I looked on it and received instruction:
A little sleep, a little slumber,
A little folding of the hands to rest;
So shall your poverty come like a prowler,
And your need like an armed man.

63. Proverbs 28:19–20, 27

He who tills his land will have plenty of bread,
But he who follows frivolity will have poverty enough!
A faithful man will abound with blessings,
But he who hastens to be rich will not go unpun-
ished. . . .
He who gives to the poor will not lack,
But he who hides his eyes will have many curses.

64. Ecclesiastes 2:26

For God gives wisdom and knowledge and joy to a man who
is good in His sight; but to the sinner He gives the work of
gathering and collecting, that he may give to him who is
good before God. This also is vanity and grasping for the
wind.

65. Ecclesiastes 3:1–2

To everything there is a season,
A time for every purpose under heaven:
A time to be born,
And a time to die;
A time to plant,
And a time to pluck what is planted.

66. *Ecclesiastes 5:10–13, 18–20*

He who loves silver will not be satisfied with silver;
Nor he who loves abundance, with increase.
This also is vanity.
When goods increase,
They increase who eat them;
So what profit have the owners
Except to see them with their eyes?
The sleep of a laboring man is sweet,
Whether he eats little or much;
But the abundance of the rich will not permit him to
sleep.
There is a severe evil which I have seen under the sun:
Riches kept for their owner to his hurt. . . .
Here is what I have seen: It is good and fitting for one to eat
and drink, and to enjoy the good of all his labor in which he
toils under the sun all the days of his life which God gives
him; for it is his heritage. As for every man to whom God
has given riches and wealth, and given him power to eat of
it, to receive his heritage and rejoice in his labor—this is the
gift of God. For he will not dwell unduly on the days of his
life, because God keeps him busy with the joy of his heart.

67. *Song of Solomon 2:4*

He brought me to the banqueting house,
And his banner over me was love.

68. *Isaiah 45:2–3*

I will go before you
And make the crooked places straight;
I will break in pieces the gates of bronze
And cut the bars of iron.
I will give you the treasures of darkness
And hidden riches of secret places,
That you may know that I, the LORD,

Who call you by your name,
Am the God of Israel.

69. Isaiah 48:17–18

Thus says the LORD, your Redeemer,
The Holy One of Israel:
"I am the LORD your God,
Who teaches you to profit,
Who leads you by the way you should go.
Oh, that you had heeded My commandments!
Then your peace would have been like a river,
And your righteousness like the waves of the sea."

70. Isaiah 55:10–11

For as the rain comes down, and the snow from heaven,
And do not return there,
But water the earth,
And make it bring forth and bud,
That it may give seed to the sower
And bread to the eater,
So shall My word be that goes forth from My mouth;
It shall not return to Me void,
But it shall accomplish what I please,
And it shall prosper in the thing for which I sent it.

71. Isaiah 60:5–6

Then you shall see and become radiant,
And your heart shall swell with joy;
Because the abundance of the sea shall be turned to you,
The wealth of the Gentiles shall come to you.
The multitude of camels shall cover your land,
The dromedaries of Midian and Ephah;
All those from Sheba shall come;
They shall bring gold and incense,
And they shall proclaim the praises of the LORD.

72. *Isaiah 61:6*

But you shall be named the priests of the LORD,
They shall call you the servants of our God.
You shall eat the riches of the Gentiles,
And in their glory you shall boast.

73. *Jeremiah 17:7–8*

Blessed is the man who trusts in the LORD,
And whose hope is the LORD.
For he shall be like a tree planted by the waters,
Which spreads out its roots by the river,
And will not fear when heat comes;
But its leaf will be green,
And will not be anxious in the year of drought,
Nor will cease from yielding fruit.

74. *Jeremiah 29:11–12*

For I know the thoughts that I think toward you, says the LORD, thoughts of peace and not of evil, to give you a future and a hope. Then you will call upon Me and go and pray to Me, and I will listen to you.

75. *Jeremiah 30:16*

Therefore all those who devour you shall be devoured;
And all your adversaries, every one of them, shall go into captivity;
Those who plunder you shall become plunder,
And all who prey upon you I will make a prey.

76. *Jeremiah 31:16–17*

Thus says the LORD:
"Refrain your voice from weeping,
And your eyes from tears;
For your work shall be rewarded, says the LORD,
And they shall come back from the land of the enemy.

There is hope in your future, says the LORD,
That your children shall come back to their own border."

77. Lamentations 3:22–33

Through the LORD's mercies we are not consumed,
Because His compassions fail not.
They are new every morning;
Great is Your faithfulness.
"The LORD is my portion," says my soul,
"Therefore I hope in Him!"
The LORD is good to those who wait for Him,
To the soul who seeks Him.
It is good that one should hope and wait quietly
For the salvation of the LORD.
It is good for a man to bear
The yoke in his youth.
Let him sit alone and keep silent,
Because God has laid it on him;
Let him put his mouth in the dust—
There may yet be hope.
Let him give his cheek to the one who strikes him,
And be full of reproach.
For the LORD will not cast off forever.
Though He causes grief,
Yet He will show compassion According to the multitude
of His mercies.
For He does not afflict willingly,
Nor grieve the children of men.

78. Ezekiel 36:26–30

I will give you a new heart and put a new spirit within you; I
will take the heart of stone out of your flesh and give you a
heart of flesh. I will put My Spirit within you and cause you
to walk in My statutes, and you will keep My judgments and
do them. Then you shall dwell in the land that I gave to
your fathers; you shall be My people, and I will be your God.

I will deliver you from all your uncleannesses. I will call for the grain and multiply it, and bring no famine upon you. And I will multiply the fruit of your trees and the increase of your fields, so that you need never again bear the reproach of famine among the nations.

79. Ezekiel 47:9

And it shall be that every living thing that moves, wherever the rivers go, will live. There will be a very great multitude of fish, because these waters go there; for they will be healed, and everything will live wherever the river goes.

80. Daniel 11:32

The people who know their God shall be strong, and carry out great exploits.

81. Hosea 6:1–3

Come, and let us return to the LORD;
For He has torn, but He will heal us;
He has stricken, but He will bind us up.
After two days He will revive us;
On the third day He will raise us up,
That we may live in His sight.
Let us know,
Let us pursue the knowledge of the LORD.
His going forth is established as the morning;
He will come to us like the rain,
Like the latter and former rain to the earth.

82. Joel 2:23–26

Be glad then, you children of Zion,
And rejoice in the LORD your God;
For He has given you the former rain faithfully,
And He will cause the rain to come down for you—
The former rain,
And the latter rain in the first month.

The threshing floors shall be full of wheat,
And the vats shall overflow with new wine and oil.
So I will restore to you the years that the swarming locust
has eaten,
The crawling locust,
The consuming locust,
And the chewing locust,
My great army which I sent among you.
You shall eat in plenty and be satisfied,
And praise the name of the LORD your God,
Who has dealt wondrously with you;
And My people shall never be put to shame.

83. Amos 5:4

For thus says the LORD to the house of Israel:
"Seek Me and live."

84. Amos 9:5–6, 13–14

The LORD God of hosts,
He who touches the earth and it melts,
And all who dwell there mourn;
All of it shall swell like the River,
And subside like the River of Egypt.
He who builds His layers in the sky,
And has founded His strata in the earth;
Who calls for the waters of the sea,
And pours them out on the face of the earth—
The LORD is His name. . . .
"Behold, the days are coming," says the LORD,
"When the plowman shall overtake the reaper,
And the treader of grapes him who sows seed;
The mountains shall drip with sweet wine,
And all the hills shall flow with it.
I will bring back the captives of My people Israel;
They shall build the waste cities and inhabit them;

They shall plant vineyards and drink wine from them;
They shall also make gardens and eat fruit from them.''

85. *Obadiah 1:17*

But on Mount Zion there shall be deliverance, And there
shall be holiness; The house of Jacob shall possess their possessions.

86. *Jonah 2:2*

And he said:
''I cried out to the LORD because of my affliction,
And He answered me.
Out of the belly of Sheol I cried,
And You heard my voice.''

87. *Micah 6:8*

He has shown you, O man, what is good;
And what does the LORD require of you
But to do justly,
To love mercy,
And to walk humbly with your God?

88. *Nahum 1:13*

For now I will break off his yoke from you,
And burst your bonds apart.''

89. *Habakkuk 2:3*

For the vision is yet for an appointed time;
But at the end it will speak, and it will not lie.
Though it tarries, wait for it;
Because it will surely come,
It will not tarry.

90. *Zephaniah 3:17*

The LORD your God in your midst,
The Mighty One, will save;

He will rejoice over you with gladness,
He will quiet you with His love,
He will rejoice over you with singing."

91. *Haggai 2:8–9*

"The silver is Mine, and the gold is Mine," says the LORD of hosts. "The glory of this latter temple shall be greater than the former," says the LORD of hosts. "And in this place I will give peace," says the LORD of hosts.

92. *Zechariah 8:12–13*

For the seed shall be prosperous,
The vine shall give its fruit,
The ground shall give her increase,
And the heavens shall give their dew—
I will cause the remnant of this people
To possess all these.
And it shall come to pass
That just as you were a curse among the nations,
O house of Judah and house of Israel,
So I will save you, and you shall be a blessing.
Do not fear,
Let your hands be strong.

93. *Malachi 3:10–12*

"Bring all the tithes into the storehouse,
That there may be food in My house,
And try Me now in this,"
Says the LORD of hosts,
"If I will not open for you the windows of heaven
And pour out for you such blessing
That there will not be room enough to receive it.
And I will rebuke the devourer for your sakes,
So that he will not destroy the fruit of your ground,
Nor shall the vine fail to bear fruit for you in the field,"
Says the LORD of hosts;

"And all nations will call you blessed,
For you will be a delightful land,"
Says the LORD of hosts.

94. *Matthew 6:19–34*

Do not lay up for yourselves treasures on earth, where moth and rust destroy and where thieves break in and steal; but lay up for yourselves treasures in heaven, where neither moth nor rust destroys and where thieves do not break in and steal. For where your treasure is, there your heart will be also. The lamp of the body is the eye. If therefore your eye is good, your whole body will be full of light. But if your eye is bad, your whole body will be full of darkness. If therefore the light that is in you is darkness, how great is that darkness! No one can serve two masters; for either he will hate the one and love the other, or else he will be loyal to the one and despise the other. You cannot serve God and mammon. Therefore I say to you, do not worry about your life, what you will eat or what you will drink; nor about your body, what you will put on. Is not life more than food and the body more than clothing? Look at the birds of the air, for they neither sow nor reap nor gather into barns; yet your heavenly Father feeds them. Are you not of more value than they? Which of you by worrying can add one cubit to his stature? So why do you worry about clothing? Consider the lilies of the field, how they grow: they neither toil nor spin; and yet I say to you that even Solomon in all his glory was not arrayed like one of these. Now if God so clothes the grass of the field, which today is, and tomorrow is thrown into the oven, will He not much more clothe you, O you of little faith? Therefore do not worry, saying, "What shall we eat?" or "What shall we drink?" or "What shall we wear?" For after all these things the Gentiles seek. For your heavenly Father knows that you need all these things. But seek first the kingdom of God and His righteousness, and all these things shall be added to you. Therefore do not worry about tomorrow, for tomorrow will worry about its own things. Sufficient for the day is its own trouble.

95. *Mark 10:17–31*

Now as He was going out on the road, one came running, knelt before Him, and asked Him, "Good Teacher, what shall I do that I may inherit eternal life?" So Jesus said to him, "Why do you call Me good? No one is good but One, that is, God. You know the commandments: 'Do not commit adultery,' 'Do not murder,' 'Do not steal,' 'Do not bear false witness,' 'Do not defraud,' 'Honor your father and your mother.' " And he answered and said to Him, "Teacher, all these things I have kept from my youth." Then Jesus, looking at him, loved him, and said to him, "One thing you lack: Go your way, sell whatever you have and give to the poor, and you will have treasure in heaven; and come, take up the cross, and follow Me." But he was sad at this word, and went away sorrowful, for he had great possessions. Then Jesus looked around and said to His disciples, "How hard it is for those who have riches to enter the kingdom of God!" And the disciples were astonished at His words. But Jesus answered again and said to them, "Children, how hard it is for those who trust in riches to enter the kingdom of God! It is easier for a camel to go through the eye of a needle than for a rich man to enter the kingdom of God." And they were greatly astonished, saying among themselves, "Who then can be saved?" But Jesus looked at them and said, "With men it is impossible, but not with God; for with God all things are possible." Then Peter began to say to Him, "See, we have left all and followed You." So Jesus answered and said, "Assuredly, I say to you, there is no one who has left house or brothers or sisters or father or mother or wife or children or lands, for My sake and the gospel's, who shall not receive a hundredfold now in this time—houses and brothers and sisters and mothers and children and lands, with persecutions—and in the age to come, eternal life. But many who are first will be last, and the last first."

96. Luke 6:38

Give, and it will be given to you: good measure, pressed down, shaken together, and running over will be put into your bosom. For with the same measure that you use, it will be measured back to you.

97. John 14:2–3, 12–14, 27–28

In My Father's house are many mansions; if it were not so, I would have told you. I go to prepare a place for you. And if I go and prepare a place for you, I will come again and receive you to Myself; that where I am, there you may be also. . . . Most assuredly, I say to you, he who believes in Me, the works that I do he will do also; and greater works than these he will do, because I go to My Father. And whatever you ask in My name, that I will do, that the Father may be glorified in the Son. If you ask anything in My name, I will do it. . . . Peace I leave with you, My peace I give to you; not as the world gives do I give to you. Let not your heart be troubled, neither let it be afraid. You have heard Me say to you, "I am going away and coming back to you." If you loved Me, you would rejoice because I said, "I am going to the Father," for My Father is greater than I.

98. Acts 4:33–35

And with great power the apostles gave witness to the resurrection of the Lord Jesus. And great grace was upon them all. Nor was there anyone among them who lacked; for all who were possessors of lands or houses sold them, and brought the proceeds of the things that were sold, and laid them at the apostles' feet; and they distributed to each as anyone had need.

99. Romans 8:28, 32, 35–39

And we know that all things work together for good to those who love God, to those who are the called according to His purpose. . . . He who did not spare His own Son, but delivered Him up for us all, how shall He not with Him also freely give us all things? . . . Who shall separate us from the love of Christ? Shall tribulation, or distress, or persecution, or famine, or nakedness, or peril, or sword?

As it is written:

"For Your sake we are killed all day long;

We are accounted as sheep for the slaughter."

Yet in all these things we are more than conquerors through Him who loved us. For I am persuaded that neither death nor life, nor angels nor principalities nor powers, nor things present nor things to come, nor height nor depth, nor any other created thing, shall be able to separate us from the love of God which is in Christ Jesus our Lord.

100. Romans 11:33–36

Oh, the depth of the riches both of the wisdom and knowledge of God! How unsearchable are His judgments and His ways past finding out!

"For who has known the mind of the LORD?

Or who has become His counselor?"

"Or who has first given to Him

And it shall be repaid to him?"

For of Him and through Him and to Him are all things, to whom be glory forever. Amen.

101. Romans 13:8

Owe no one anything except to love one another, for he who loves another has fulfilled the law.

102. First Corinthians 4:2

Moreover it is required in stewards that one be found faithful.

103. Second Corinthians 8:1–15

Moreover, brethren, we make known to you the grace of God bestowed on the churches of Macedonia: that in a great trial of affliction the abundance of their joy and their deep poverty abounded in the riches of their liberality. For I bear witness that according to their ability, yes, and beyond their ability, they were freely willing, imploring us with much urgency that we would receive the gift and the fellowship of the ministering to the saints. And not only as we had hoped, but they first gave themselves to the Lord, and then to us by the will of God. So we urged Titus, that as he had begun, so he would also complete this grace in you as well. But as you abound in everything—in faith, in speech, in knowledge, in all diligence, and in your love for us—see that you abound in this grace also. I speak not by commandment, but I am testing the sincerity of your love by the diligence of others. For you know the grace of our Lord Jesus Christ, that though He was rich, yet for your sakes He became poor, that you through His poverty might become rich. And in this I give advice: It is to your advantage not only to be doing what you began and were desiring to do a year ago; but now you also must complete the doing of it; that as there was a readiness to desire it, so there also may be a completion out of what you have. For if there is first a willing mind, it is accepted according to what one has, and not according to what he does not have. For I do not mean that others should be eased and you burdened; but by an equality, that now at this time your abundance may supply their lack, that their abundance also may supply your lack— that there may be equality. As it is written, "He who gathered much had nothing left over, and he who gathered little had no lack."

104. Second Corinthians 9:6–11

But this I say: He who sows sparingly will also reap sparingly, and he who sows bountifully will also reap bountifully. So let each one give as he purposes in his heart, not grudgingly or of necessity; for God loves a cheerful giver. And God is able to make all grace abound toward you, that you, always having all sufficiency in all things, may have an abundance for every good work.

As it is written:

"He has dispersed abroad,

He has given to the poor;

His righteousness endures forever."

Now may He who supplies seed to the sower, and bread for food, supply and multiply the seed you have sown and increase the fruits of your righteousness, while you are enriched in everything for all liberality, which causes thanksgiving through us to God.

105. Galatians 3:13

Christ has redeemed us from the curse of the law, having become a curse for us (for it is written, "Cursed is everyone who hangs on a tree").

106. Galatians 6:6–10

Let him who is taught the word share in all good things with him who teaches. Do not be deceived, God is not mocked; for whatever a man sows, that he will also reap. For he who sows to his flesh will of the flesh reap corruption, but he who sows to the Spirit will of the Spirit reap everlasting life. And let us not grow weary while doing good, for in due season we shall reap if we do not lose heart. Therefore, as we have opportunity, let us do good to all, especially to those who are of the household of faith.

107. Ephesians 1:3

Blessed be the God and Father of our Lord Jesus Christ, who has blessed us with every spiritual blessing in the heavenly places in Christ,

108. Ephesians 6:2–3

"Honor your father and mother," which is the first commandment with promise: "that it may be well with you and
you may live long on the earth."

109. Philippians 4:6, 13, 19

Be anxious for nothing, but in everything by prayer and
supplication, with thanksgiving, let your requests be made
known to God. . . . I can do all things through Christ who
strengthens me. . . . And my God shall supply all your
need according to His riches in glory by Christ Jesus.

110. Colossians 3:1–2

If then you were raised with Christ, seek those things which
are above, where Christ is, sitting at the right hand of God.
Set your mind on things above, not on things on the earth.

111. First Thessalonians 5:12–13

And we urge you, brethren, to recognize those who labor
among you, and are over you in the Lord and admonish
you, and to esteem them very highly in love for their work's
sake. Be at peace among yourselves.

112. Second Thessalonians 3:3

But the Lord is faithful, who will establish you and guard
you from the evil one.

113. First Timothy 5:8

But if anyone does not provide for his own, and especially
for those of his household, he has denied the faith and is
worse than an unbeliever.

114. First Timothy 6:7–12, 17–19

For we brought nothing into this world, and it is certain we
can carry nothing out. And having food and clothing, with
these we shall be content. But those who desire to be rich

fall into temptation and a snare, and into many foolish and harmful lusts which drown men in destruction and perdition. For the love of money is a root of all kinds of evil, for which some have strayed from the faith in their greediness, and pierced themselves through with many sorrows. But you, O man of God, flee these things and pursue righteousness, godliness, faith, love, patience, gentleness. Fight the good fight of faith, lay hold on eternal life, to which you were also called and have confessed the good confession in the presence of many witnesses. . . . Command those who are rich in this present age not to be haughty, nor to trust in uncertain riches but in the living God, who gives us richly all things to enjoy. Let them do good, that they be rich in good works, ready to give, willing to share, storing up for themselves a good foundation for the time to come, that they may lay hold on eternal life.

115. Second Timothy 2:20–21

But in a great house there are not only vessels of gold and silver, but also of wood and clay, some for honor and some for dishonor. Therefore if anyone cleanses himself from the latter, he will be a vessel for honor, sanctified and useful for the Master, prepared for every good work.

116. Titus 2:12

Teaching us that, denying ungodliness and worldly lusts, we should live soberly, righteously, and godly in the present age.

117. Philemon 1:6

that the sharing of your faith may become effective by the acknowledgment of every good thing which is in you in Christ Jesus.

118. Hebrews 11:1

Now faith is the substance of things hoped for, the evidence of things not seen.

119. Hebrews 13:15–16, 20–21

Therefore by Him let us continually offer the sacrifice of praise to God, that is, the fruit of our lips, giving thanks to His name. But do not forget to do good and to share, for with such sacrifices God is well pleased. . . . Now may the God of peace who brought up our Lord Jesus from the dead, that great Shepherd of the sheep, through the blood of the everlasting covenant, make you complete in every good work to do His will, working in you what is well pleasing in His sight, through Jesus Christ, to whom be glory forever and ever. Amen.

120. James 1:17

Every good gift and every perfect gift is from above, and comes down from the Father of lights, with whom there is no variation or shadow of turning.

121. First Peter 2:9

But you are a chosen generation, a royal priesthood, a holy nation, His own special people, that you may proclaim the praises of Him who called you out of darkness into His marvelous light.

122. First Peter 3:12–13

For the eyes of the LORD are on the righteous,
And His ears are open to their prayers;
But the face of the LORD is against those who do evil.''
And who is he who will harm you if you become followers of what is good?

123. Second Peter 1:3

As His divine power has given to us all things that pertain to life and godliness, through the knowledge of Him who called us by glory and virtue.

124. First John 3:22

And whatever we ask we receive from Him, because we keep His commandments and do those things that are pleasing in His sight.

125. First John 5:14–15

Now this is the confidence that we have in Him, that if we ask anything according to His will, He hears us. And if we know that He hears us, whatever we ask, we know that we have the petitions that we have asked of Him.

126. Second John 4–6

I rejoiced greatly that I have found some of your children walking in truth, as we received commandment from the Father. And now I plead with you, lady, not as though I wrote a new commandment to you, but that which we have had from the beginning: that we love one another. This is love, that we walk according to His commandments. This is the commandment, that as you have heard from the beginning, you should walk in it.

127. Third John 1:2

Beloved, I pray that you may prosper in all things and be in health, just as your soul prospers.

128. Jude 20–21

But you, beloved, building yourselves up on your most holy faith, praying in the Holy Spirit, keep yourselves in the love of God, looking for the mercy of our Lord Jesus Christ unto eternal life.

129. Revelation 21:1–7

Now I saw a new heaven and a new earth, for the first heaven and the first earth had passed away. Also there was no more sea. Then I, John, saw the holy city, New Jerusalem, coming down out of heaven from God, prepared as a bride adorned for her husband. And I heard a loud voice from heaven saying, "Behold, the tabernacle of God is with men, and He will dwell with them, and they shall be His people. God Himself will be with them and be their God. And God will wipe away every tear from their eyes; there shall be no more death, nor sorrow, nor crying. There shall be no more pain, for the former things have passed away." Then He who sat on the throne said, "Behold, I make all things new." And He said to me, "Write, for these words are true and faithful." And He said to me, "It is done! I am the Alpha and the Omega, the Beginning and the End. I will give of the fountain of the water of life freely to him who thirsts. "He who overcomes shall inherit all things, and I will be his God and he shall be My son.

By meditating on these precious promises and passages, you are about to embark on a great adventure. The apostle Paul declared in 2 Corinthians 1:20, emphasis added, "For all the promises of God in Him are Yes, and in Him Amen, to the glory of God through us." Our Father in heaven is a good Father who is *always* true to His Word.

Notes

Chapter 1

1 Healing Medley, "Nothing Is Impossible" by Ralph Carmichael, 1977, Outfield Music; "One Touch" by Bonnie Plunkett, 1970, Gospel Publishing House; "I Expect a Miracle Today" by Sharon Daugherty, Daugherty Ministries, Inc.

2 *U.S. News & World Report*, 11 December 1995. *U.S. News/* Bozell poll of 1,009 adults conducted by KRC Research 3–7 November 1995, with consulting by *U.S. News* pollsters Celinda Lake of Lake Research and Ed Goeas of the Tarrance Group.

3 "Making Ends Meet—Is It Getting Tougher? Or Are We Just Getting Softer?" (interview with Bruce Howard, Ph.D., Judith Briles, Ph.D., and Gene Frost, Jr., Ed.D.), *Marriage Partnership*. Also noted: "Money is the No. 1 cause of marriage breakups," Griffin said. "We need to be very scrupulous and disciplined and Christian about how we handle our money. Money is dangerous" (Dan Griffin as quoted in "Managing Money Termed Biblically Based Idea," by Terri Lackey, copyright 1995 Baptist Press).

4 Orville Scott, "Stewardship Book Suggests Fewer Carry Financial Load," Baptist Press, 27 March 1995.

5 Helen Lee, "Churches Battle Downward Donations," *Christianity Today*, News Section, 24 April 1995.
6 *BridgeBuilder*, January/February 1989, 30.
7 R. T. Kendall, *Tithing: A Call to Serious Biblical Giving* (Grand Rapids, Mich.: Zondervan, 1982), 27.
8 Ibid., 21.
9 Matthew Henry, as quoted in *Thoughts on Prosperity: Thoughts and Reflections from History's Great Thinkers*, The Forbes Leadership Library (Chicago: Triumph Books, 1996), 81.

Chapter 3

1 R. T. Kendall, *Tithing*, 82.
2 George Muller, *The Autobiography of George Muller*, (Springdale, Penn.: Whitaker House, 1984), 197.
3 Kenneth L. Barker, "First Fruits," *Kindred Spirit*, Spring 1988.

Chapter 5

1 "The Longer I Serve Him" by William J. Gaither, 1965, Gaither Music Company.

Chapter 7

1 Kendall, *Tithing*, 106–7.

Chapter 8

1 Kendall, *Tithing*, 18.
2 Barker, "First Fruits."
3 "Making Ends Meet—Is It Getting Tougher? Or Are We Just Getting Softer?" (Interview with Bruce Howard, Ph.D., Judith Briles, Ph.D., and Gene Frost, Jr., Ed.D., *Marriage Partnership* magazine.
4 Kendall, *Tithing*, 103
5 Ibid., 88.

6 Charles Caldwell Ryrie, *Balancing the Christian Life* (Chicago, Moody, 1969), 86.

7 Kendall, *Tithing,* 59–60.

Chapter 9

1 "Lamb of Glory." Words by Phil McHugh and Greg Nelson, 1982 by Shepherd's Fold Music/River Oaks Music (Tree Group).

Chapter 10

1 Kendall, *Tithing,* 52.

2 Ibid., 41.

3 R. Laird Harris, Gleason L. Archer, Jr. and Bruce K. Waltke, eds. *The Theological Wordbook of the Old Testament,* Vol 1 (Chicago: Moody, 1980), 170.

Chapter 11

1 "Nothing Is Impossible" by Ralph Carmichael.

2 *Ministry Currents,* January-March 1992, 5.

3 Ron Blue, *Ten Things Every Pastor Should Know About Money* (:Leadership Dynamics International, 1986), 3–4.

4 A dear friend of mine in the ministry, David Crank, has written a book entitled *God Finances and the Bible Way to Pay Off Your Home,* which has helped me see the importance of the concept of the "storehouse."

5 *Thoughts on Prosperity,* 69.

Chapter 12

1 "Nothing Is Impossible" by Ralph Carmichael.

Bibliography

Barker, Kenneth L., "First Fruits", *Kindred Spirit*, Spring, 1988.

Blomberg, Craig, *I Corinthians: The NIV Application Commentary*, Grand Rapids, Mich.: Zondervan, 1994.

Blue, Ronald W., *Ten Things Every Pastor Should Know About Mondy*, Leadership Dynamics International, Inc., 1986.

Gangel, Kenneth O., "How Should We Then Give?", *Kindred Spirit*, Spring, 1988.

Kendall, R. T., *Tithing: A Call to Serious Biblical Giving*, Grand Rapids, Mich.: Zondervan, 1982.

Muller, George, *The Autobiography of George Muller*, Springdale, Penn.: Whitaker House, 1984.

Ryrie, Charles Caldwell, *Balancing The Christian Life*, Chicago: Moody, 1969.

Wiersbe, Warren W., *Be Obedient*, Wheaton, Ill.: Victor Books, A division of Scripture Press Publications, Inc., 1991.

Henry, Matthew, *Thoughts on Prosperity: Thoughts and Reflections from History's Great Thinkers*, Chicago: Triumph Books, 1996.

Resources

There are many fine teaching resources available to give you detailed help in the area of financial planning and budgeting. I've selected three that I believe you'll find especially helpful.

Blue, Ron. *Master Your Money: A Step-By-Step Plan for Financial Freedom.* Nashville: Thomas Nelson Publishers, 1991.

Blue, Ron & Judy. *Raising Money-Smart Kids: How to Teach Your Children the Secrets of Earning, Saving, Investing, and Spending Wisely.* Nashville: Thomas Nelson Publishers, 1992.

Blue, Ron. *Master Your Money Workbook: A Step-By-Step Plan for Getting Your Money Matters Under Control and Achieving Financial Security.* Nashville: Thomas Nelson Publishers, 1993.

About the Author

Mega bestselling author, pastor, and healing Evangelist Benny Hinn has been used by God to bless throughout the world through his teaching and preaching of the Word of God. Millions of people across the world have come to know the Holy Spirit in Person, power, and presence of the Holy Spirit through his writing and teaching.

A native of Israel who immigrated to Canada as a teenager, he is the founder of the World Outreach Center, a rapidly-growing church in Orlando, Florida, with over 7,000 members. Tens and hundreds of thousands of people attend his crusades and conferences in North America and around the world to experience Benny's dynamic teaching and the power of the Holy Spirit.

His daily and weekly television broadcasts are beamed literally around the world, touching millions of people each week. He is the author of the international bestsellers, *Good Morning Holy Spirit*, *The Anointing*, and *Welcome, Holy Spirit*.